A PHILOSOPHER LO
ARCHITECTURE

What should our buildings look like? Or is their usability more important than their appearance? Paul Guyer argues that the fundamental goals of architecture first identified by the Roman architect Marcus Vitruvius Pollio – good construction, functionality, and aesthetic appeal – have remained valid despite constant changes in human activities, building materials, and technologies, as well as in artistic styles and cultures. Guyer discusses philosophers and architects throughout history, including Alberti, Kant, Ruskin, Wright, and Loos, and surveys the ways in which their ideas are brought to life in buildings across the world. He also considers the works and words of contemporary architects including Annabelle Selldorf, Herzog and de Meuron, and Steven Holl, and shows that – despite changing times and fashions – good architecture continues to be something worth striving for. This new series offers short and personal perspectives by expert thinkers on topics that we all encounter in our everyday lives.

PAUL GUYER is Jonathan Nelson Professor of Humanities and Philosophy at Brown University. He is the author of numerous books on Kant and aesthetics, including *Knowledge, Reason, and Taste: Kant's Response to Hume* (2008) and the three-volume *A History of Modern Aesthetics* (Cambridge, 2014).

A Philosopher Looks at

In this series, philosophers offer a personal and philosophical exploration of a topic of general interest.

Books in the series

A PHILOSOPHER LOOKS AT

ARCHITECTURE

PAUL GUYER

CAMBRIDGE
UNIVERSITY PRESS

CAMBRIDGE
UNIVERSITY PRESS

University Printing House, Cambridge CB2 8BS, United Kingdom

One Liberty Plaza, 20th Floor, New York, NY 10006, USA

477 Williamstown Road, Port Melbourne, VIC 3207, Australia

314–321, 3rd Floor, Plot 3, Splendor Forum, Jasola District Centre, New Delhi – 110025, India

79 Anson Road, #06–04/06, Singapore 079906

Cambridge University Press is part of the University of Cambridge.

It furthers the University's mission by disseminating knowledge in the pursuit of education, learning, and research at the highest international levels of excellence.

www.cambridge.org
Information on this title: www.cambridge.org/9781108820424
DOI: 10.1017/9781108907019

First published 2021

Printed in the United Kingdom by TJ Books Limited, Padstow Cornwall

A catalogue record for this publication is available from the British Library.

ISBN 978-1-108-82042-4 Paperback

CONTENTS

CONTENTS

LIST OF FIGURES

Figures appear between pages 97 and 98.

Introduction

W e begin with two weekend houses, the Villa Rotonda by the Italian Renaissance architect Andrea Palladio (1508–80) and the Y-House by the contemporary American architect Steven Holl (b. 1947) (Figures 1 and 2). Built more than four centuries apart – the Villa Rotonda was completed over more than twenty-five years from 1565 to 1592,[1] while the Y-House was completed much more quickly, in 1999 – the two houses could not look more different. The older building, constructed like all of Palladio's work out of stucco-covered brick, is a liberal transformation of an ancient temple – the Pantheon in Rome built by the Emperor Hadrian and dedicated around 126 CE – into a private home for which there is no known antecedent in antiquity. Its remarkable geometry begins with an interior rotonda surrounded by rectangular rooms within a perfect square set within an imaginary circle. The circumference of this circle passes through the center-point of the porticos before each of the four matched faces of the house, and each of the porticos has six Ionic columns supporting a triangular pediment crowned with statuary. Similar statues crown the walls that flank the broad flights of steps leading from the ground to the porticos and the main level of the house. The Y-House, by contrast, is an asymmetrical version of the letter, with a short stem and two arms of unequal length, as different from Palladio's symmetrical plan as could be. Sheathed in horizontal tongue-and-groove wood

1

siding painted barn-red, it has all-glass walls at the ends of the two arms of the Y and small windows asymmetrically placed on the other walls of the house. The first house is unmistakably from the Italian Renaissance, the other unmistakably from the turn of the twenty-first century.

There are other differences between them, which reflect further differences between the periods in which they were built: the Villa Rotonda stands atop a small hill a short distance outside of the contemporaneous city limits of the northern Italian city of Vicenza where Palladio did much of his work, and it could be easily reached from the town on foot or by horse or wagon; while the Y-House is located several hours north of New York City with a vista of the Catskill Mountains, but is easily reached by the ubiquitous modern means of transportation – the car. No doubt there are socio-economic differences between the owners as well: the one house built by wealthy Italian gentlemen, their wealth coming from the Church or the land; the other built for a contemporary upper-middle-class nuclear family, their wealth coming from some contemporary business or profession, with corresponding differences in use, the one originally used for weekend gatherings with other wealthy magnates, the later house no doubt being primarily used for family weekend or summer vacation retreats from the usual routine of work and school, perhaps with occasional visits from other family members or close friends.[2]

Nevertheless, beneath the superficial differences between these two buildings there are deeper similarities. I picked two examples of the same building type: the secondary home intended to be used for weekends or vacations. (I chose the Villa Rotonda because, unlike many of Palladio's other villas, it was not the headquarters of a working farm, flanked by wings for agricultural equipment and produce.) This means that there must be some similarities in the way the buildings were or are used despite all the socio-economic and cultural differences between sixteenth-century Vicenza and twentieth- and twenty-first-century New York state. Both houses were meant for pleasant retreats from the city. Both houses are situated to afford their residents pleasant vistas of nature and easy access to it. Both houses take best advantage of their sites: the Villa Rotonda is rotated 45 degrees from a straight north–south axis (or, since it is a square within a circle, a straight north–south–east–west orientation) so that every room will be lit by the sun at some point in the day; the Y-House has its largest glass areas facing northeast to get the best view while also minimizing excessive glare and solar gain. Holl's description of the experience of light in the Y-House is just as valid for the Villa Rotonda: "The slow passing of time from early morning to sunset is to be a primary experience in the house as different areas of the house become activated by the movement of the sun."[3] Both houses have a well-defined distinction between public and private spaces: The central rotonda and largest rooms of the Villa Rotonda served for the entertainment of larger groups, while the smaller rooms would have afforded more private spaces for sleeping or dining without guests. The public living and dining spaces of the Y-House and its bedrooms are separated on the two levels of the two arms of the Y. And so on.

But beneath this there is an even deeper level of similarity. First, although the building materials and technologies of Renaissance Italy and contemporary North America are certainly different, both architects exploited the technologies available to them as best they could: Palladio using brick, stone, stucco and plaster, and advances in the construction of domes to create the remarkable interior spaces and external facades, porticoes, and steps of the building; Holl using large sheets of glass unavailable centuries earlier but also steel and concrete to create the open entrance hall of the house, and contemporary heating, ventilation, and air-conditioning (HVAC) equipment, lighting, wiring, and more. Both architects were no doubt trying to accommodate the needs expressed or assumed by the owners for relaxing, entertaining, sleeping, and cooking (although in the Villa Rotonda this would not have been done by the owners and in the Y-House probably is), although certainly the owners' conceptions of their needs – the programs for the houses, in architects' terminology – would have been discussed with the architect and modified and refined as the plans were developed. And certainly in both cases the architects were concerned with how the houses would look, from outside and inside, from closer and further away, at different times of day and night, and during different seasons of the year, perhaps seen as one physical object in a larger landscape but also as an image in a woodcut or engraving or photograph. Both architects would have been concerned with how the materials of the house would feel, what would be smooth and what rough, how conversation, laughter, and music would sound in or among the rooms of the house, and more.

In other words, both the Renaissance and the contemporary architects would have been concerned with how their structures would be built, how they would be used, and how they would be experienced.

The argument of this book will be that for all the changes over the years and centuries in architectural technologies and styles and in cultural and socio-economic conditions, at the most abstract level the core goals and values of architecture have not changed. Architects have always been and will continue to be concerned with how and how well their buildings can be and are built, how well they serve the needs of the client, and how pleasing, engaging, and/or interesting the experience of the building will be for its audience, which may include owners, other users, and those who may simply see their buildings, whether on foot, from cars or other vehicles, or through images in various media from prints to photos to computer screens. These three fundamental goals were identified in the oldest surviving treatise on architecture in the Western canon, the *Ten Books on Architecture* by Marcus Vitruvius Pollio (ca. 70–20 BCE). Vitruvius stated that all buildings "must be executed in such a way as to take account of durability, utility, and beauty" (*firmitas, utilitas,* and *venustas*), or, as in another translation, "durability, convenience, and beauty."[4] Works of architecture are structures that are built to please us by both their utility or convenience and their appearance (in the broadest possible sense, appealing not only to sight but to our other senses as well). And they are to be built out of sound and enduring materials put together well so that they can accomplish the first two goals, typically for a long time although sometimes architects are called upon to design structures such as platforms for special events and pavilions for expositions that must be safe but are not intended to last. Here Vitruvius's three Latin terms will be translated as good construction, functionality, and aesthetic appeal. These are not literal translations, but they will be used to stress the generality of these goals. As available materials and structural technologies, as ways of life and therefore conceptions of appropriate uses thereof, and as aesthetic expectations – what might be found beautiful or grand or exciting – have varied radically through history, the general values of good construction, functionality, and aesthetic appeal remain constant. Likewise, as more particular architectural theories, for example the view that elements of construction should be masked by surfaces covered with painting and sculpture, gave way to the view that aesthetic appeal should be achieved by construction alone, for instance by the exposure of steelwork or the imprint of the wooden forms used in pouring concrete, those general values remain valid. I will argue this here by looking at a sample of philosophical treatments of architecture, architectural theories, and actual buildings from antiquity to the present, concluding with a glimpse into the future.

Three comments before I start. First, it is easy to get confused about the extreme generality of the Vitruvian categories, or, to put the point another away, it is easy to get confused about the difference between philosophy of architecture and architectural theory. For example, the architectural historian Kenneth Frampton has written that the analysis of architecture by the nineteenth-century

architect and theorist Gottfried Semper (1803–79) in terms
of four elements – namely hearth (heat-source), earthwork
(elevation above the ground and therefore protection from
water, animals, and other humans), a framework/roof (and
therefore protection from sun and rain), and an enclosing
membrane (and therefore privacy) – "represent[s] a fundamental break with the Vitruvian triad of *utilitas, firmitas,*
[and] *venustas.*"[5] No, Semper's list of the elements of architecture does not conflict with the Vitruvian goals of good
construction, utility, and aesthetic appeal; rather it specifies
the basic *parts* of buildings *by means of which* they must
realize both their functionality and their beauty and which
therefore must be well-designed and built for those goals to
be achieved in an enduring way – for example a hearth must
be well-designed and built of good stone or brick in order to
both draw well and look good for a long time. Semper's
architectural theory operates one level down from the
Vitruvian ideals, or is a theory of the means to the
Vitruvian ends. Frampton, who conceives of "tectonics" as
the "poetics of construction," is particularly interested in the
modernist ideal of achieving beauty through structure rather
than by surface materials or ornamentation, but this does
not deny the importance of aesthetic appeal as one of the
fundamental aims of architecture to be achieved, along with
functionality, through interesting as well as good construction. One of the subjects of Frampton's work is the
nineteenth-century British ecclesiastical architect Augustus
Welby Northmore Pugin (1812–52). Frampton cites Pugin as
stating "First, that there should be no features about a
building which are not necessary for convenience,

construction or propriety; second, that all ornament should consist of the enrichment of the essential construction of the building."[6] But again it is a mistake for him to then describe Pugin as "Anti-Vitruvian and anti-utilitarian to the same degree."[7] Pugin was hardly opposed to utility or functionality, since he explicitly made "convenience and propriety" necessary conditions for architecture, where propriety can itself be understood as the appearance of a building's suitability for its intended use, thus as part of its utility. But neither was he opposed to beauty: he just thought that ornament should come from the "essential construction" of the building, not from something more superficial. In other words, Pugin thought that both utility and aesthetic appeal should be achieved *through* good construction: he accepted the Vitruvian ideals, but had a particular view of how they should be realized.

Second, my argument is not that the three goals of good construction, functionality, and aesthetic appeal *define* architecture; they apply to any of the arts or technologies that human beings have developed to fulfill our practical needs – *technai* in the original Greek sense.[8] If we take the traditional list of basic human needs – food, clothing, and shelter – the Vitruvian goals apply to those too. We want our food to be nourishing, of course, that is, functional; but also appealing in both taste and appearance, that is, aesthetically appealing; and to be properly prepared – washed, salted, cooked, etc. – to be safe to be consumed now or later, in other words to be well-made. We want our clothing to be functional, whether that be concealing or revealing, depending on the occasion on which it is to be worn – warm or cool depending on the season; to be attractive, although fashion and therefore what counts as attractive may change quickly or slowly; and to be made of good materials and well-constructed, although again what will count as satisfying that goal will vary with the intended function of the garment – a party dress may not have to be constructed to last but must be in fashion, while a coat or shoes may have to transcend current fashion fads but be well-made out of enduring materials. In all these cases, the goals of good construction, functionality, and aesthetic appeal will have to be met in some way. Architecture specifically might be defined, as for example by John Ruskin (1819–1900), as "the art which so disposes and adorns the edifices raised by man, for whatsoever uses, that the sight of them may contribute to his mental health, power, and pleasure."[9] Then it is the reference to edifices raised by human beings that distinguishes architecture from other arts, whereas the explicit requirements that architecture serve various human uses but also provide aesthetic pleasure, and the underlying assumption that its products should be adequately designed and constructed to serve these dual purposes, are something that architecture shares with the other arts.[10] That architecture concerns the construction, function, and aesthetics of human structures may be taken as the definition of the discipline, while the statement that architecture aims at the *good* construction, *successful* function, and aesthetic *appeal* applies general norms, ideals, or values of human artifice to the case of architecture.

Third, in order to realize the Vitruvian ideals architecture need not be restricted to a specific list of building types, such as private residences (the examples with which I began), or places of public gathering such as temples, courts, markets, and theaters. Obviously the list of building types with which architects might be concerned has changed over the ages. Vitruvius himself did not discuss office parks and airports, nor are city walls or temples a large part of any architect's practice today.[11] But sometimes people draw a distinction between purely functional structures, which can be left to engineers, and genuine architecture, which aims at more than mere functionality; indeed, the nineteenth-century philosopher Arthur Schopenhauer (1788–1860) went so far as to assert that insofar as architecture makes "provision for useful purposes" it is not a fine art at all.[12] We will come back to his claim later (see p. 74). The point now is that even if we do make a distinction between purely functional structures of engineering and works of genuine architecture that aim at some kind of aesthetic appeal as well as functionality, this distinction would not correspond to any neat division of building types; any structure can count as a work of architecture if it aims at aesthetic appeal as well as functionality. One celebrated work by the contemporary architect Annabelle Selldorf (b. 1960) is the Sunset Park Material Recovery Facility (2013), "a processing center for New York City's curbside metal, glass and plastic recyclables undertaken by Sims Municipal Recycling and the City of New York" (the clients) on the Brooklyn waterfront (Figure 3). Perhaps many recycling facilities and trash transfer stations are designed solely by civil engineers, and no doubt there were civil engineers involved in Selldorf's project. But the "master plan," which includes "a tipping building, where recyclables arrive by barge and truck; processing and bale-storage buildings; and an administrative and education center" and pedestrian bridge, arranges "buildings to support functionality, creates distinct circulation systems to separate visitors from operations, and adds 2 acres of native plantings," is clearly a work of architecture (and landscape architecture). Aspects of the buildings go beyond strict functionality, such as the glass walls of the administrative and education center, which provide magnificent views of the rest of the East River waterfront, while the vast roof that extends over both the shed for the reception of the materials and the dock where barges arrive, while fully functional, is also clearly angled for aesthetic impact as well as for shedding water. The project is functional in various ways: in addition to being designed for convenient unloading, packing, and transferring of materials, it also uses recycled materials throughout, and "includes one of the largest applications of photovoltaics in New York" and a "wind turbine," which should keep costs of operation down. But it also aims at aesthetic appeal: that recycled materials are used throughout might have kept costs down but also expresses the purpose of the facility, an aesthetic consideration, while that "structural elements are inverted to appear on the exterior, giving steel girders and lateral bracing a greater visual impact" is an aesthetically appealing effect.[13] The project was designed for both functionality and aesthetic appeal, and uses constructional technology both to ensure that those two goals will be served for a long time and to contribute directly to the beauty of what would otherwise be a purely utilitarian complex. Whatever other recycling facilities might be like, this one is definitely a work of architecture that realizes the three Vitruvian ideals.

In this essay I am not going to attempt to define aesthetic appeal or consider the question of whether architecture should count as a fine art.[14] I am going to focus on the continuing validity of the perennial triad of architectural values. My argument will proceed in four chapters. The first chapter will expound the development of the analysis from Vitruvius through the Renaissance architect and writer Leon Battista Alberti (1404–72) and architect Andrea Palladio to the eighteenth-century Scottish philosopher Henry Home, Lord Kames (1696–1782) and the architectural theorist Marc-Antoine Laugier (1713–69). The second chapter will focus on the expansion of the category of aesthetic appeal from a traditional conception of *beauty* to include the aesthetic expression of *meaning*, looking at ideas from Immanuel Kant (1724–1804) at the end of the eighteenth century and his follower Schopenhauer at the beginning of the nineteenth, through those of John Ruskin and Gottfried Semper in the middle of the nineteenth century. The third chapter will consider how the ideas of several twentieth-century philosophers such as Susanne Langer (1895–1985) and Roger Scruton (1944–2020) and practicing but theoretically inclined architects such as Steen Eiler Rasmussen (1898–1990), Grant Hildebrand (b. 1934), and Steven Holl fit into the Vitruvian scheme. Finally, the fourth chapter will look at how some works as well as theoretical statements of Frank Lloyd Wright (1867–1959), Adolf Loos (1870–1933), and Ludwig Mies van der Rohe (1886–1969), different as both the buildings and words of those architects are from those of earlier generations, still fit into the scheme. A brief fifth chapter, "Looking Forward," will argue that the Vitruvian triad will remain valid through all the challenges architecture can be expected to face in the future.

Finally, a personal word. My father was an artist who made his living as an illustrator and advertising art director but who also exhibited his paintings, and painted until his death at almost ninety-six. On the basis of my performance on an elementary school aptitude test, my mother formed the idea that I should be an architect, and arranged for her best friends to give me some books on architecture as bar mitzvah gifts, books that I still treasure and one of which I will even cite later on. In junior high school I took courses in mechanical and architectural drafting. But I also started reading philosophy in high school, and wanted a liberal arts education before getting a professional education in architecture. So I did not go straight from high school to an undergraduate program in architecture, but instead went to college with both architecture and philosophy in mind as possible careers. My first year in college I had two wonderful philosophy teachers, Stanley Cavell and Rogers Albritton, and an incompetent calculus teacher, supposedly a prerequisite for going to architecture school later. When I took my first course on Kant the next year (with a very young Robert Nozick), the die was cast in favor of architectonics rather than architecture. I have continued to look at and read about architecture, but had no formal training in the subject after my junior high school course. Unlike many philosophers of mathematics who may have started off as mathematicians, or philosophers of science who may have started off as physicists or biologists, I make no pretense to have been trained as an architect, an architectural theorist, or an architectural historian. If I was ever properly trained in anything at all, it was as an historian of philosophy. This book is just my reflection on architecture as an historian of philosophy and philosopher bringing his way of thinking to a field that he loves.

This book will certainly not be a work of architecture that would have fulfilled my mother's ambition for me, but I dedicate it to the memory of Betty Rubenstein Guyer anyway. And I would like to thank my wife, Pamela Foa, for many helpful suggestions for this book and judicious criticism of the manuscript.

1 Good Construction, Functionality, and Aesthetic Appeal

From Vitruvius to the Eighteenth Century

1 Vitruvius

Marcus Vitruvius Pollio (ca. 70–20 BCE) apparently drew on a rich legacy of Greek texts on building, all now lost. His own *Ten Books on Architecture*[1] begins with the recommendation that architects be well-educated in mathematics, including music, and philosophy, including natural science. But most of it is devoted to matters such as the proper choice and preparation of building materials, siting, and proper design for infrastructure, such as ports, markets, and fortifications, for public buildings such as temples, and for private homes – in other words, to his categories of good construction and functionality. What is necessary for aesthetic appeal receives only a brief explicit description in Book I of *De architectura*. Brief as it is, his words are pregnant with possibilities for future thought about architecture. But before we turn to Vitruvius's accounts of construction, functionality, and aesthetic appeal, let's look at his general view about the relation between human life and the rest of nature, for that is the foundation for much of the rest.

The importance of this relationship is evident from Book I, chapter i, on the education of the architect. Following his statement of the importance of philosophy

15

for the architect and then of music as the science of harmonies, thus including mathematics, Vitruvius next mentions the importance of "medicine," also very broadly understood, "because of the problems posed by the latitude ... , by the properties of the air, by locations which are healthy or infected, and by water use; for without such knowledge no healthy house can be built." Architects must understand astronomy in order to take account of the directions of wind and light. They "should also know the mandatory legal regulations for the construction of buildings with party walls, for the distribution of eaves and sewers, and of windows and water-pipes around buildings ... so that, before starting buildings, they can ensure that no legal disputes are left for householders."[2] These statements show that Vitruvius understands architecture as a fundamental medium for the relation of human beings to the rest of nature and to each other in society. The products of architecture are not simply aesthetic objects, in our terminology, intended for pleasurable contemplation, but are also means for the interactions of people with their physical and social environments on which the possibility of human life and flourishing depends. Facilitating human flourishing in its natural and social context is the underlying goal of the architect, whether designing a house, a fort, or a temple, and that is why the architect must be steeped in every form of human knowledge. Of course, if aesthetic satisfaction is part of human flourishing along with the satisfaction of the more practical goal of shelter, then the architect must aim at both aesthetic appeal and functionality as that which is to be achieved through good construction.

16

Vitruvius's naturalism is the background for his evolutionary account of "The Origin of Buildings" in Book ii, chapter i.[3] Vitruvius is famous for the image of the "primitive hut," the idea that early humans sought shelter from the elements under canopies of leaves and boughs, and learned to mimic such rough shelters with a simple structure of four corner-posts supporting beams and rafters that could be covered with roofs and walls of thatch and mud.[4] The idea that all architecture has its origin in the primitive hut persisted into the eighteenth and nineteenth centuries.[5] But Vitruvius actually offered a more sophisticated account of the origin of building types. He supposed that early humans were first drawn to form groups larger than nuclear families by the attraction of fire, invented languages once they had formed into groups "by indicating frequently the things they used,"[6] and then began to create shelters suited to the particular environments in which they found themselves, using the materials they found in those environments to imitate naturally occurring kinds of shelter that they observed.

> It was then that some of them from these first groups began to make shelters of foliage, others to dig caves at the foot of mountains and yet others to build refuges of mud and branches in which to shelter in imitation of the nests of swallows and their way of building. Next, by observing each other's shelters and incorporating the innovation of others in their own thinking about them, they built better kinds of hut day by day.[7]

For example, "in Gaul, Spain, Lusitania and Aquitaine, houses are roofed with oak shingles or thatched" because those materials are abundant, but "the Phrygians, who live on the plains, have very little timber," so instead "choose natural mounds, and cutting trenches through the middle and digging out passages, enlarge the interior space as much as the nature of the site allows."[8] Vitruvius thus saw human beings as adapting to their natural environment by both imitation and invention: they imitate what they find in nature but also what they find in each other, and they invent to improve upon both. Human beings exist in complex interaction with each other and with the rest of nature, and architecture is a fundamental medium of such interaction, as, although Vitruvius does not mention this, the equally fundamental human arts of cooking and dressing also are. Those too use materials afforded to us by nature, that is, whatever particular environment some population happens to find itself in, but in ways that can begin with crude imitations of nature – wearing the pelts of animals much as the animals themselves did – and then can be radically transformed by the human capacities for invention (turning flax into linen or cellulose into rayon) and imitation (fashion). One particular form of imitation that Vitruvius subsequently notes is the imitation of features of timber construction in stone: "Starting from . . . components of carpentry, builders adapted them for the relief work of the stone and marble structures of sacred buildings." For example, no doubt following long tradition, he interprets the triglyphs of the Doric temple frieze as imitations of the painted ends of timber joists.[9] But the imitation of wood in stone is hardly the entire origin of architecture; human beings are too adaptive and too inventive for that.

It is against this background of imitative yet invent-ive adaptation to nature and society that Vitruvius conducts his discussion of good construction and functionality in the form of the description of building materials, construction methods, and building types that occupies most of *De archi-tectura* (until he comes to the discussion of sundials, water clocks, and military machinery such as catapults that occu-pies the final two of his ten books). His exploration of human adaptation to nature in architecture begins with accounts of the proper siting of individual rooms, whole cities, and types of structures such as temples within cities in Book I. Even before he introduces his trio of the funda-mental goals of architecture he notes that "appropriateness to nature will be observed if the light for bedroom and libraries is derived from the east, for bathrooms and winter apartments from the west, for picture galleries and rooms which require steady light from the north." The last, he explains, is because "that zone of the sky is not dazzled or obscured by the trajectory of the sun, but the light remains constant all day long";[10] in an era before alarm clocks bed-rooms should be lit from the east so that the morning light will awaken sleepers, libraries also lit from the east because before gas or electric lighting reading was best done in the morning, and bathrooms and winter apartments should face west because they will be warmest in the afternoon. The orientation of whole houses should also be "correctly planned if ... we take careful notice of the regions and latitudes of the world in which they are to be built," thus "It is clear that houses in the north should be roofed over, as closed as possible and provided with few apertures," while "houses in southern regions under the impact of the sun should be provided with more apertures and face north and northeast because those regions are oppressed by heat."[11] The agglomerations of houses that form towns and cities should be sited "in a high place, without mists or frost, and exposed to weather conditions that are neither sweltering nor freezing, but temperate"; "proximity to marshy terrain is to be avoided" before modern mosquito control;[12] and "harbours present great advantages if they are naturally well placed and have prominent headlands or projecting promontories" to keep ships and therefore travel and commerce safe from storms.[13] Architects must also understand the directions of the winds in different locations, at different times of day, and in different seasons, in order to maximize healthy breezes and minimize unhealthy or destructive winds.[14] Finally, "the selection of areas in the city with respect to their development for communal use ... for sacred buildings, the forum and other communal spaces" must be based on the "convenience of the citizens."[15] These are all instances of functionality, which must be understood broadly as the facilitation of the adaptation of human beings to nature and to each other for the successful execution of such activities and tasks as sleeping, bathing, reading, trading, and worshiping, which are part although not the whole of human flourishing.

      Intelligent adaptation to nature is also the underlying theme of Vitruvius's account of solid and durable construction, which takes the form of a description of the proper selection and preparation of building materials and the proper techniques for building with them. This is the focus of Book II of *De architectura*. Following the historical account of the different types of shelter that emerged in different environments already noted, the next chapter introduces the elements water, fire, air, and earth as the basis for Vitruvius's attempt at a scientific explanation of the properties of various materials, thus of their strengths and weaknesses and therefore best uses.[16] His explanations may seem archaic to us, but his recommendations are obviously rooted in generations of experience and are sound. For example, he describes the best types of clay for making bricks and how long they need to be cured as well as the different shapes of Greek and Roman bricks;[17] the best sands and the preparation of lime for making mortar;[18] the preparation of pozzolana, a type of concrete made from tufa, the lava found around Mounts Vesuvius and Etna, which can harden underwater;[19] and different types of stone, the locations of the quarries where they may be found, and how long they must rest between quarrying and building.[20] He then describes the different ways in which walls should be laid with either brick or stone, and how they should be mortared and filled. His focus is primarily on the strength and endurance of walls, a vital matter at a time in which every city and not merely every military installation was surrounded by walls. But he also touches upon aesthetic issues, observing that *opus reticulatum*, or construction from irregular stones rather than repeated courses of uniform bricks or stones, may be "the more attractive of the two, but it is apt to form cracks because it comprises disconnected bed- and vertical joints in all parts of the wall,"[21] and also on political matters, as when he observes that sometimes even kings who could afford to build with quarried stone or marble should "not turn up their noses at structures made with brick walls."[22] Although functionality and aesthetic appeal may be separate goals, sometimes they can be achieved together through good construction, and sometimes one may have to be traded off with the other. Then Vitruvius turns to timber. He explains the properties of different woods such as fir, various oaks, alder, ash, and many others, in terms of their proportions of earth, air, fire, and water. His science may be outdated, but his advice on the best ways to harvest timber and the best uses of different types are well-grounded in human experience: such as the use of fir for flooring that will stay straight,[23] alder for foundation piles,[24] and larch, which "is known only in those municipalities along the banks of the river Po and on the shores of the Adriatic," for its resistance to rot, grubs, and fire.[25] "Consequently those who can follow the advice contained in this body of instructions will be better informed and equipped to choose how to use the particular types for construction."[26] Throughout, Vitruvius's aim has been to explain how human beings can intelligently adapt the materials afforded to them by nature, wherever they may find themselves and whatever that material may be, to achieve both functionality and aesthetic appeal.

Having completed his discussion of the conditions of good construction in Book II, Vitruvius turns to the discussion of different building types, from temples to aqueducts, which occupies Books III through VIII. His emphasis through much of this discussion is on the conditions for maximizing the utility of these different types, such as the forum, basilica, treasuries, prisons, theaters, harbors, and shipyards (Book v), private homes (Book vi), and even pavements (Book vii). We have already seen how this discussion goes from the preliminary examples of siting and orientation in Book i. But Vitruvius's discussion of building types begins with the temple in Books iii and iv, and here not only utility but also beauty are at issue. So at this point a return to Vitruvius's general comments about the sources of aesthetic appeal in Book i is in order.

Although the topic of beauty loomed large in modern aesthetics – one of the definitions of the field offered by its founder, Alexander Gottlieb Baumgarten, was as *ars pulcre cogitandi*, the art of thinking beautifully[27] – and remained central until quite recently, Vitruvius's treatment of the aesthetic aspects of architecture (*venustas*) is brief compared to his treatments of construction and functionality. It might also seem to be confined to a formalistic approach equating aesthetic appeal with the proportions within and among the parts of a building, such as the columns considered both singly and as forming its colonnades and porticoes, indeed with proportions strictly governed by particular mathematical ratios; at least that is how Vitruvius's approach to aesthetic appeal was so understood by successors such as the Renaissance humanist Leon Battista Alberti, the Renaissance architect Andrea Palladio, and perhaps twentieth-century masters such as Le Corbusier and Mies van der Rohe. But Vitruvius's conception of the beauty of buildings is more complex than that. First, although he does speak of proportions in mathematical terms, he also emphasizes that what is crucial to beauty is how the parts of buildings *appear* to human observers from normal vantage-points, not strict conformity to ideal ratios in themselves. His account of beauty is anthropocentric in a second sense: the most crucial ratios in architecture, for example the ratio between the diameter and the height of columns, are determined by the proportions of the human body, in this case that between the height of a person and the length of a foot. Further, these proportions vary in relation to different types of human bodies, as in Vitruvius's analogy between the proportions of Doric, Ionic, and Corinthian columns and those of the figures of men, matrons, and maidens (for further discussion, see pp. 30–32 below).[28] And these analogies, as well as the use of even more representational elements in architecture, can give buildings meaning and relate them to human emotions. So Vitruvius recognizes *content* as well as *form* as contributing to the aesthetic appeal of architecture. The recognition that buildings may have *meaning* in various ways as well as pleasing by the *forms* of the parts and wholes will be a significant development in the subsequent history of the aesthetics of architecture.

In Book 1, chapter ii, on "The Principles of Architecture," Vitruvius enumerates a series of terms that seem to convey a formalistic conception of beauty, although they also touch upon matters of utility on the one hand and of aspects of meaning on the other. They also reflect Vitruvius's recognition of architecture as an intermediary between human beings and the rest of nature and among human beings in society. How to distinguish the significance of these terms and even how to translate them is not

obvious; Vitruvius himself presents several of them as translations of Greek terms. In the older translation of Morris
Hicky Morgan, the principles are Order (*ordinatio*, in
Greek *taxis*), Arrangement (*dispositio*, *diathesis*), Eurythmy
(*eurythmia*), Symmetry (*symmetria*), Propriety (*decor*), and
Economy (*distributio*, *oikonomia*);[29] in the newer and in this
case perhaps eccentric translations of Richard Schofield, the
six principles are planning, projection, harmony, modularity, appropriateness, and distribution.

Planning or order might seem to concern the
proper layout of a building for its intended function, but
in this case Vitruvius seems to have a formal foundation
for beauty in mind, since he defines this principle as
"adapting each individual element of a building to the
right dimensions and establishing its overall proportions
by reference to modularity," as Schofield translates, or in
Morgan's translation giving "due measure to the members
of a work considered separately, and symmetrical agreement to the proportions of the whole."[30] Both translators
agree that this means selecting a "module" from the elements or members of the building (in the first instance, the
radius of its columns at their base) and then designing the
whole building through mathematical functions of this
module. An obvious illustration of this requirement will
be the way in which within each order the radius of a
column is related to its overall height and the height of its
base and capital, as well as the proper height of the
architrave above and the distance between one column
and the next (intercolumniation). Although one could
also say that the intended size of the building overall will

determine the proper height of its columns and therefore their diameter, as well as the right number of them for the porticoes (four, six, eight) and in turn the right number for the lateral colonnades (seven, eleven, fifteen), all of these values will vary conjointly. Order or arrangement is an interrelation, in which the parts determine the whole but the whole also determines the parts.

Vitruvius's next principle, "arrangement" or "projection," is doubly ambiguous. First, while it seems to continue the previous principle, concerning "the appropriate placement of a building and the elegant completion of the work, based on a combination of the parts appropriate to the characteristics of the work,"[31] or, in Morgan's translation, the "character" of the work, the last term might bring in meaning or content: if it means that the design of a building should be appropriate to its intended function, for example as a temple as opposed to a courthouse, then order or arrangement is more than a purely formal or mathematical consideration. Second, Vitruvius continues in a way that seems to concern *plans* or *drawings* rather than physical buildings: in Schofield's translation, he says that the "types of projection" are "ground-plan" (*ichnographia*), "orthogonal elevation" (*orthographia*), and "perspectival drawing" (*scaenographia*) – this is why Schofield translates *dispositio* as "projection" rather than "arrangement."[32] It seems strange that Vitruvius should switch from talking about properties of buildings to kinds of drawings, but perhaps we could take him to be using the three kinds of drawings to suggest that the architect must be concerned with the proper layout of a building, with the design of its elevations, and in particular with how those will appear from the perspectives from which the building will actually be viewed, as well as with the overall impression the building will make from the likely points of view on it. He could be talking about buildings themselves by talking about the ways of drawing them.

Vitruvius's third principle explicitly concerns aesthetic appeal. Eurythmy or harmony "consists of a beautiful appearance and harmonious effect deriving from the composition of the separate parts," and is "achieved when the heights of the elements of a building are suitable to their breadth, to their length."[33] This seems to concern the overall dimensions of a building rather than the relation between its parts. But Vitruvius continues that this principle is satisfied "when all the elements match its modular system," which seems much the same as the previous principle of planning or order. And it seems much the same as the fourth principle as well, "the appropriate agreement of the components of the building itself and the correspondence of the separate parts to the form of the whole scheme based on one of those parts selected as the standard unit," for example, the radius of a column that determines so many other dimensions of the building's parts and whole. Schofield translates *symmetria* as "modularity" rather than by its traditional cognate "symmetry" precisely because this requirement does not concern bilateral symmetry, like that of the left and right sides of a human body, but rather concerns the relation between the one canonical dimension or measurement and all the other dimensions of a building. Vitruvius uses the human body as an illustration of his conception of modularity, supposing that there are relations among the dimensions of members such as fingers, palms, and forearms such that the size of any one determines the proper size of the others, but at this stage he does not suggest that the proper ratios among the dimensions of elements of buildings and of the parts to the whole building have any direct relation to the canonical dimensions of human bodies and their parts. For the moment his conception of the overlapping principles of order, harmony, and modularity seems purely mathematical. He seems to be suggesting that beauty lies in certain mathematical relationships.

Nonmathematical considerations come into play, however, with Vitruvius's remaining categories of *decor*, appropriateness or propriety, and distribution or economy. The former also bears on "perfect appearance," but arises from "following a rule" given by "custom or nature" rather than mathematics. And appropriateness according to custom adds a dimension of content to the thus far formalistic account of architectural beauty: "One follows a rule when roofless buildings open to the sky are built to Jupiter, Creator of Lightning," although apparently this conception of Jupiter as well as the association with this feature of buildings is only a matter of custom; it is also custom that "Doric temples should be dedicated to Minerva, Mars, and Hercules, since it is appropriate to provide buildings without elaborate ornament for these deities because of their warlike character," while "Temples of the Corinthian order built for Venus, Flora, Proserpina, the God of the Springs and of the Nymphs will clearly have the right characteristics, because, given the gentleness of these deities, more graceful and florid buildings decorated with leaves and volutes will clearly enhance the appearances appropriate to them."[34] Buildings built on the Doric or Corinthian order do not strike us as beautiful just because of their mathematical ratios, although those are part of their beauty, but because, by custom, their appearance seems appropriate to the meaning of a building, as a temple to a particular god or goddess. "Appropriateness in accordance with custom is [also] demonstrated when, for example, suitable and elegant vestibules [match] magnificent interiors," while it is violated when, for example, elegant interiors are found inside shabby exteriors. That would be jarring for almost anyone, although perhaps finding it inappropriate for "dentils to be carved in the cornices of Doric entablatures" depends on expectations based on more specific customs.[35] The aesthetic appeal of buildings depends on aspects of meaning in the broadest sense as well as of form.

Appropriateness with regard to nature rather than custom can also bear on utility rather than beauty, for it is under this heading that Vitruvius states that "very healthy" and well-watered sites should be chosen for sanctuaries and makes his remarks about the proper direction of light for rooms with different functions.[36] Utility is also Vitruvius's first concern with the principle of distribution or economy, which consists in "the appropriate management of resources and the site, and the prudent control of finances during construction thanks to careful calculation."[37] Economy in this sense is obviously the efficient use of time, capital, and labor, to use modern terms, and although an architect or a client may certainly take pleasure in knowing that a project has been completed efficiently, it has nothing directly to do with the appearance of the finished product. Economy may be a part of functionality that does not bear directly on aesthetic appeal.

Finally, Vitruvius mentions a "second level" of distribution or economy, which consists in planning buildings differently for rich or powerful people, for urban or country estates, and for moneylenders or senators; "in brief, the layouts of buildings must be appropriate to each class of person."[38] This kind of economy is sometimes just a matter of utility, as when a country villa needs wings for storage of grain, animals, and equipment that a townhouse does not, or a politico needs large reception rooms while a financier may need smaller rooms for discreet deal-making. But it might also be a matter of appearance, as when the home of a politician should demonstrate his power while that of a financier should downplay his wealth. This would not be a question of pure form, but more a matter of content, or of perceived congruence between the appearance of a building and its intended function.

The Vitruvian conception of the aesthetic appeal of architecture thus involves more than purely formal beauty grounded in mathematical ratios alone. And even the formal aspect of architectural beauty is, as previously observed, anthropomorphic as well as mathematical. First, the connection between modularity in the human body and in architecture is not just an analogy for Vitruvius – the thought that "if nature has composed the human body so that its individual limbs correspond proportionately to the whole figure," it would also be a good idea that individual components of buildings "should be exactly commensurable with the configuration of the whole structure"[39] – but is something more direct. It also goes beyond the fact that "the ancients" derived their "system of mensuration ... from members of the body," that is, derived units such as inches, feet, and cubits from the typical sizes of human fingers, feet, and forearms.[40] Rather, they used the proportions among the parts of the human body to determine the proper proportions among the parts of architectural elements and among the elements in a building. Thus "they fixed six as the perfect number because a man's foot is a sixth of his height,"[41] and then developed the proportions of the Doric column and all the other parts on that ratio: "When they discovered that a man's foot is the sixth of his height, they applied that unit to the column and allocated six times the diameter they had established for the bottom of the shaft to its height, including the capital" (later measurements have shown that the ratio of base diameter to height in Doric columns is typically closer to 1:7). This "is why the Doric column began to exhibit the proportions, strength and grace of the male body in buildings," thus assuring both the adequacy of the columns to bear their heavy loads (functionality) and the "beauty of their appearance" (aesthetic appeal).[42] The proportions of the other two main orders of columns, the Ionic and the Corinthian, were then developed on the basis of the more graceful proportions of the Greek matron and the downright willowy figure of maidens, "who are endowed with more graceful limbs because of their tender age."[43] Even more direct mimesis of the human body is supposed to explain the volutes of the Ionic capital "like graceful curls hanging down from the hair" and the "flutes down the whole trunk

31

[of the column] like the folds in the robes traditionally worn by married women,"[44] while the Corinthian capital is explained as a representation of acanthus leaves springing up from the grave of a young girl through a basket that her nurse had left above it, a legend no doubt already old in Vitruvius's day.[45]

The second aspect of anthropomorphism that modifies any initial suggestion that the proper form of architectural elements and edifices as wholes is determined by mathematical ratios alone is Vitruvius's recognition that such forms must be modified to take account of conditions under which the buildings are actually observed. These conditions include the angles and distances from which those things are actually seen, as well as atmospheric effects. For example, "the upper diameters" of columns "should be enlarged to compensate for the increasing distances for the glance of the eye as it looks up,"[46] "corner columns should be made thicker than the rest by a fiftieth of their own diameter, because they are strongly silhouetted against the air and appear more slender to observers,"[47] the "level of the stylobate [platform for columns] must be adjusted so that it curves upward ... for if it is laid absolutely horizontally, it will look concave to the eye,"[48] and

> the further up the gaze of the eye has to climb, the less easily can it penetrate the density of the air; and so it falters when the height is great, and ... transmits to the senses an unreliable estimate of the dimensions of the modules. For this reason, one must always incorporate in the calculations an increase in the size of the components worked out according to the modular system.[49]

As Vitruvius sums up, "our sight searches for beauty, and if we do not satisfy its desire for gratification by increasing proportions with additions derived from modules in order to correct false impressions with appropriate adjustments, the building will present an awkward and clumsy sight to onlookers."[50] The modular system is not governed by mathematics alone, but by the conjunction of mathematics with the facts of human perception – another way in which architecture mediates between human beings and nature. This is an insight that had to be recovered long after the text of Vitruvius had itself been rediscovered.

A final point about anthropomorphism concerns a direct use of the human figure in architectural design, namely the Caryatids, that is, statues of female figures used as columns in the Erechtheum at the Acropolis, the treasuries at Delphi, and other sites.[51] Vitruvius's story is that these were representations of women taken as slaves after the defeat of the Peloponnesian city of Caria, which had allied itself with the Persians, and that the victorious Greeks led by Athens subsequently "devised images of them placed in load-bearing positions in public buildings so that the punishment of the crime of the Carians would be known to posterity and remain in history."[52] Such a story is why the architect has to know history. In a case like this we can regard the building or its part as having a literal meaning, the assertion "You will regret making war on us." This may not be a beautiful message, but in such cases it may be presented in a manner that contributes to the overall aesthetic impact of the work, an element of content that clearly goes beyond pure form. But such a message should also be considered a special case: even if some buildings do, it would be a mistake to assume that every building must present a message or content that can be grasped in concepts and translated into words.

The three Vitruvian ideals of good construction, functionality, and aesthetic appeal were highly general and interpreted flexibly by their original author. Let us look now at how these concepts were interpreted in the Renaissance and beyond.

2 Alberti and Palladio

Leon Battista Alberti (1404–72) could stand for the entire Italian Renaissance as much as any other single figure.[53] Born in Genoa as the son of an exiled Florentine merchant, he studied letters and law at Padua and Bologna, then took holy orders and spent much of his life in the employ of the Vatican but was also welcome at the humanist courts of Ferrara and Urbino. He had vast humanistic learning but was also a productive mathematician and even a cryptographer. He began his treatise *Della pittura* (On painting), chiefly on optics and perspective, in 1435, and then turned his attention to architecture. His treatise on architecture, *De re aedificatoria* (On building), was circulating in Latin by 1450, published in Italian as early as 1456, and finally posthumously printed in Latin in 1486. But Alberti was also a practicing and consulting architect: he restored a Roman aqueduct for Pope Nicolas V, and planned the ideal Renaissance city of Pienza for the humanist Pope Pius II, Aeneas Silvius Piccolomini. His own architectural works included a facade for the Palazzo Rucellai in Florence and the transformation of the partially completed Gothic facade of Santa Maria Novella into a Renaissance masterpiece; the transformation of the Gothic Tempio Malatestiano in Rimini into another Renaissance monument; and above all the Basilica of Sant'Andrea in Mantua, the facade of which is a triumphal arch that ties the Renaissance back to the glory of the Roman Empire. In all these cases Alberti apparently confined himself to the design of the work and left details and supervision of its construction to others, although *De re aedificatoria* demonstrates extensive knowledge of construction materials and techniques, or at least extensive knowledge of the literature on the subject including Vitruvius but also Theophrastus, Pliny, and others.

Alberti's work is obviously modeled on and draws from that of Vitruvius. In form, Alberti follows Vitruvius in dividing his work into ten books, and in substance, he reproduces the Vitruvian triad; speaking of the six elements of building, which he classifies as locality, *area* or overall plan and perimeter, compartition or division into rooms, and walls, roofs, and openings, Alberti writes:

> their individual parts should be well suited to the task
> for which they were designed, and above all, should be
> very commodious; as regards strength and endurance,
> they should be sound, firm, and quite permanent; yet
> in terms of grace and elegance, they should be
> groomed, ordered, garlanded, as it were in their every
> part. Now ... we have set down the roots and
> foundations of our discussion ...[54]

Alberti is clearly employing Vitruvius's three categories of good construction, functionality, and aesthetic appeal. In terms of organization, he also follows Vitruvius's pattern of beginning with an account of sound materials and construction techniques, although he amplifies Vitruvius's account with material from other ancient authors, and he similarly follows that with discussions of the various types of building, although he usefully replaces the Roman's discussion of clocks and military machinery with a detailed discussion of machines used in construction itself, such as pulleys, hoists, and cranes (Book VI). However, there are also two important differences between Alberti's approach and that of Vitruvius.

The first and perhaps more obvious is that he largely replaces Vitruvius's empiricist – perhaps Epicurean and Lucretian – approach to the relation between humanity and nature with a more rationalist – Pythagorean and Platonic – conception of the order of nature and its necessary reflection in architectural design. This is evident in both Alberti's general statements and his treatment of particular subjects. In the most general terms, Alberti defines beauty, the third Vitruvian category, as *concinnitas*, the "reasoned harmony of all the parts within a body, so that nothing may be added, taken away, or altered, but for the worse," and he then states that this is an "inherent property, to be found suffused all through the body of that which may be called beautiful," to which ornament is strictly secondary, "a form of auxiliary light and complement" that may highlight the formal beauty of the work but does not make an essential contribution to it.[55] Alberti further insists that *concinnitas*, his own coinage that there is no point in translating, is not to be "judged by variable and relative criteria,"[56] but is actually a mathematically determinate relationship:

> Beauty is a form of sympathy and consonance of the parts within a body, according to definite number, outline, and position, as dictated by *concinnitas*, the absolute and fundamental rule in Nature. This is the main object of the art of building, and the source of her dignity, charm, authority, and worth.[57]

And because beauty consists in an objective, determinate mathematical relationship, "When you make judgments of beauty, you do not follow mere fancy, but the workings of a reasoning faculty that is inborn in the mind . . . . That is why when the mind is reached by way of sight or sound, or any other means, *concinnitas* is instantly recognized."[58] This is what makes Alberti a rationalist, rather than, like Vitruvius, an empiricist: the basis of beauty is recognized by our reason, not by feeling and certainly not by mere custom, as the older author so often suggested. And what makes Alberti's view Pythagorean and Platonic is that he assumes that the mathematical relationship that constitutes *concinnitas* and beauty is the essence of nature itself: "Neither in the whole body nor in its parts does *concinnitas* flourish as much as it does in nature itself; thus I might call it the spouse of the soul and of reason."[59] Our appreciation of mathematical structure in buildings is appreciation of the order of nature itself. Alberti makes his allegiance to Pythagoras explicit: having described several numerical relationships favored by architects, he continues that

> For us, the outline is a certain correspondence between
> the lines that define the dimensions, one dimension being
> length, another breadth, and the third height. The
> method of defining the outline is best taken from those
> objects in which Nature offers herself to our inspection
> and admiration as we view and examine them. I affirm
> again with Pythagoras: it is absolutely certain that Nature
> is wholly consistent. That is how things stand.[60]

A preference for certain ratios is not a contingent feature of human psychology; our pleasure in these ratios in architecture is rather a rational response to the essential order of the universe itself. Such a thought is often seen as the core of Renaissance Neo-Platonism, identified with such figures as Marsilio Ficino (1433–99), but Alberti traces it back to Pythagoras – a genealogy to which Plato himself would have had no objection.

We can see Alberti applying his mathematical rationalism to particular cases. As in Vitruvius, an account of the orders of columns is an essential part of Alberti's treatise. And like Vitruvius, he begins with an anthropomorphic account of the origins of the orders:

> The shapes and sizes for the setting out of columns, of
> which the ancients distinguished three kinds according to
> the variations of the human body, are well worth
> understanding. When they considered man's body, they
> decided to make columns after its image. Having taken
> the measurements of a man, they discovered that the
> width, from one side to the other, was a sixth of the
> height, while the depth, from navel to kidney, was a
> tenth . . . . The ancients may have built their columns to
> such dimensions, making some six times their base,
> others ten times.

Thus originated the heights of the Doric and Corinthian columns. But on Alberti's view the ancient designers of the orders did not long remain content with such obvious anthropomorphism. Rather, they quickly corrected mere imitation with higher mathematics. First, they divided the difference between six and ten, and "made a column eight times the width of the base, and called it Ionic"; then they corrected the dimensions of the Doric column:

> They took the lesser of the two previous terms, which was six, and added the intermediate term of the Ionic, which was eight; the sum of this addition was fourteen. This they divided in half, to produce seven. They used this number for [the correct height of] Doric columns, to make the width of the base of the shaft one seventh of the length. And again they determined the still more slender variety, which was called the Corinthian, by adding the intermediate Ionic number to the uppermost extreme and dividing the sum in half: the Ionic number being eight, and the uppermost extreme ten, the two together came to eighteen, half of which was nine. Thus they made the length of the Corinthian column nine times the diameter at the base of the shaft, the Ionic eight times, and the Doric seven. So much for this.[61]

Alberti does not argue that actual measurements have shown that the ratio of diameter to length in Doric columns is closer to 1:7 than it is to 1:6, or suggest a psychological argument that the more slender column just looks more pleasing to us; rather it is a matter of pure mathematics. Apparently it is just rational to prefer the result of these mathematical calculations to any other basis for establishing the proper proportions of columns, because after all such proportions are the order of nature itself.

There are a few places where Alberti acknowledges the kind of adjustments to purely mathematical forms required by the actual conditions of human perception that Vitruvius had emphasized. Alberti acknowledged but at the same time distanced himself from the need for such corrections when he observed that while "Some maintained that the bottom [of a column] should be one and a quarter times as thick as the top," "Others, realizing that objects appear smaller, the further they are from the eye, sensibly decided that with a tall column the top should not be reduced as much as with a short column,"[62] that "columns seem narrower in the open air than in an enclosed space" and should be adjusted accordingly, and that "the number of flutes may increase the apparent thickness of a column."[63] But these are just "certain matters relevant to [the] systems of columns that must not be overlooked," not anything essential to them; and when he comes to the real mathematics of columns in Book IX that we have just described, he makes no mention at all of these departures from his formulas. The essence of beauty lies in mathematics, not in the physiology of perception. This is the triumph of Alberti's rationalism over Vitruvius's empiricism even within his acceptance of the Vitruvian framework of architectural ideals.

Alberti's other main departure from Vitruvius is that his entire discussion of the orders of columns and the systems of design that depend on them takes place after he has announced a turn to the topic of ornament in Book VI.

This might seem like a trivial difference in organization, but it may have had significant implications for the subsequent history of architecture itself. Alberti starts Book VI by saying that he has already dealt with the "lineaments, the materials for construction, the employment of workmen, and anything else that might seem relevant to the construction of buildings" in the first five books, and that everything that comes next deals merely with the appropriate ornament for various building types (even though his discussion of construction machinery actually comes in the present book).[64] But his relegation of the discussion of columns to mere ornament was already evident in his opening statement that the fundamental elements of buildings are location, plan, partition, walls, roofs, and openings (windows and doors) – columns were not on this list. Vitruvius had started his discussion of building types with the temple, and because of this had started his discussion of building elements with columns; but Alberti starts his whole discussion of temples and therefore of columns only in Book VII, thus after his turn to ornament. This could show that the temple is not as central to a modern list of building types as it was to the ancient, and this seems reasonable enough, especially since the western Christian Church seems to have been based more on the ancient model of the basilica, a secular public building type for governmental functions, than on the ancient temple. Alberti's use of the ancient triumphal arch as the form for the facade of his own Sant'Andrea also suggests a connection between the modern church and ancient secular forms rather than the form of the temple. More generally, Alberti's treatment of columns as mere ornament may open the way to a modern conception of a building as the enclosure of a volume of space by floor, walls, and roof and of access to it by means of doors and windows in place of an ancient conception of a building as a structure of columns supporting beams, as much a sculpture as an enclosure, and just as plausibly open to the sky as roofed over, or, as emerged in Rome, a series of arches and spandrels, again either open (as in a colosseum) or roofed over. On the new conception of buildings, the proportions of the volume and its enclosure would be more significant than the proportions of columns, even rooted as the latter are in pure mathematics.

This would open the way to a greater emphasis on and variety in the overall shapes of buildings that we see over subsequent centuries, in building types with no clear classical antecedents such as the seventeenth-century additions of the Louvre or the variations of configuration illustrated at the turn of the nineteenth century by Jean-Nicolas-Louis Durand (1760–1834)[65] and the varied shapes of contemporary skyscrapers – Chippendale cabinets, lipstick tubes and pickles – and of the Sydney Opera House by Jørn Utzon, the free-form museums of Frank Gehry, and the new Barnes Collection in Philadelphia by Tod Williams and Billie Tsien. At the same time, the relegation of the column to the status of mere ornament opened the way to a use of columns liberated from ancient building types even when they continued to be a prominent element of buildings, as they did not only from the Italian Renaissance through the Greek Revival movement of the first part of the nineteenth century but also into the stripped-down Roman classicism of both fascist and democratic states in the 1930s. For just one example, while another polymath, the Frenchman Claude Perrault (1613–88), wrote a treatise explicitly entitled *Ordonnance for the Five Kinds of Columns after the Method of the Ancients* (1683) in which he explored the mathematics of the five orders of columns (Doric, Ionic, and Corinthian plus Tuscan and Composite) in even more detail than Alberti had,[66] his own masterwork, the east facade of the Louvre, deployed a two-story high colonnade of paired columns sitting on single pedestals themselves resting on the lower story of the building, which is without ancient precedent. It is a modern, primarily ornamental invention without an indispensable structural function, which, although this may be to compare the sublime to the ridiculous, can be seen as having prepared the way for the purely decorative use of ancient forms or references to them in such 1980s post-modernist buildings as those of Michael Graves. Sometimes the organization of a book means more than first appears.

One final point that might be noticed about Alberti's book is that although he deployed the traditional distinction between form and *matter*, thus between design and construction materials (analogous to his epochal distinction between outline or design [*disegno*] and color in his book on painting),[67] he did not acknowledge even to the extent that Vitruvius did the way buildings may have *content* and that content as well as form may contribute to their aesthetic interest and appeal. The concept of meaning would not become central to architectural aesthetics until the end of the eighteenth century, and would then flower in the nineteenth. Before we turn to later authors, however, a word about Palladio.

Palladio may have been the single most influential architect who ever lived: his urban style was imitated in Britain by Inigo Jones, his country villas inspired countless houses throughout Britain and North America from the eighteenth century through the first part of the twentieth (and "Palladian" windows still appear in "McMansions" today), and through the brilliant Prussian architect Karl Friedrich Schinkel (1781–1841) his plans even influenced a modern master like Mies van der Rohe. Unlike Alberti, Palladio was not born into a wealthy, educated environment; he started off as a stonemason and builder, but was taken up by a circle of wealthy humanists in Vicenza – even given the name "Palladio" by them, perhaps in honor of Pallas Athena[68] – and acquired his profound knowledge of antique building through visits to Rome funded by his patrons. But this did not lead to a slavish imitation of antique buildings or building types; on the contrary, working in three main building types – his Vicenzan urban palazzi such as the Chiericati (ca. 1550–57) and the Valmarana (1565–71), his numerous suburban and country villas throughout the Veneto, and his two great Venetian churches, San Giorgio Maggiore (1564–80) and Il Redentore (1576–80) – Palladio used the elements of ancient buildings, the columns in their several orders, porticoes and pediments, in entirely original compositions.

But where Palladio did follow precedent was in his adoption of the mathematical rationalism of Alberti. To be sure, Palladio was seriously concerned with functionality, thus his country villas were designed as both showcase houses for wealthy landowners and the headquarters of working farms,[69] an urban palazzo like the Chiericati carefully integrated public and private spaces, and Il Redentore was precisely designed to accommodate the annual procession celebrating the delivery from a plague that it had been built to commemorate.[70] And Palladio was obviously concerned with solid construction; although built with simple plastered brick, with proper maintenance many of his villas are still in excellent condition, and with more expensive materials his churches are as magnificent today as they must have been when first completed. But above all Palladio achieved beauty through geometry. In the Introduction, we saw how the Villa Rotonda was designed as a circle inscribed in a square inscribed within a larger circle, the perimeter of which passes precisely through the center-point of each of its four porticoes – a geometrical exercise unprecedented in the history of architecture but blessed by Alberti's Pythagoreanism. The Villa Rotonda is a suburban rather than agricultural villa, and thus has no flanking outbuildings, but in many of Palladio's country villas, the outbuildings flanked a perfectly square residential block, which in turn contained a central hall with three rooms on each side, in descending proportions, from front to back, typically 3:2, 2:2, and 2:1. James Ackerman's brilliant descriptions of the parallels between these ratios and musical harmonies as understood in the Renaissance shows how in his practice of aesthetics Palladio followed the ideals of Alberti.[71] But as Ackerman points out, Palladio went even further than Alberti's recommendations, and integrated the ceiling heights as well as length and breadth of rooms into his geometrical harmonies; in one example he discusses, the Palazzo Iseppo Porto (1552), Palladio designed a central hall on the *piano nobile* (main floor) that was 30 by 40 feet with a ceiling height of 30 feet, flanked by side rooms of 30 by 20 feet with 20 foot high ceilings. For all of Palladio's influence in Britain, as we will shortly see, the analogy between architectural and musical harmony and in particular this incorporation of ceiling heights into the geometrical scheme were criticized on the sort of empirical, physiological grounds that Vitruvius himself had originally noted.

This detail aside, Palladio's architectural principles remained well within the original Vitruvian paradigm of good construction realizing both functionality and aesthetic appeal, the latter in his case itself achieved through geometrical as well as decorative means. Let us now look at two examples of eighteenth-century thought to show how the Vitruvian paradigm was maintained even as Albertian-Palladian rationalism was criticized – there may be an internal debate about how to achieve aesthetic appeal, but not a rejection of it as an ideal.

3 Kames and Laugier

This section will discuss just two mid-eighteenth-century figures, one a philosopher and one an architectural theorist, to illustrate the continuing power of the Vitruvian framework even as its very general terms are variously applied.[72] Neither was anything close to a trained or practicing architect. Henry Home, Lord Kames (1696–1782), was a prominent Scottish jurist who also wrote voluminously in moral philosophy, history, and aesthetics, and was an intimate of other leading figures of the Scottish Enlightenment such as David Hume and Adam Smith. The architectural theorist is Marc-Antoine Laugier (1713–69), first a Jesuit and then a Benedictine abbé, who published his *Essay on Architecture* in 1753 and then wrote on music and on the history of Venice as well as serving on diplomatic missions. But both had interesting things to say about architecture.

In his three-volume *Elements of Criticism*, first published in 1762 and remaining in use well into the nineteenth century, Kames devoted a chapter to "Gardening and Architecture." In a general work on what we may find pleasing in all the arts but which is primarily concerned with the emotional impact of literature, when he comes to architecture Kames touches upon the requirement of *firmitas*, or good construction, only in passing. But he takes it as given that architecture is concerned with both functionality and aesthetic appeal, or, in his terms, utility and ornament. Buildings and their parts can be divided into "three kinds, namely, what are intended for utility solely, what for ornament solely, and what for both," although most works of architecture fall into the last group and therefore the great challenge for architects, or "difficulty of contrivance, respects buildings that are intended to be useful as well as ornamental."[73] And when it comes to beauty, although Kames does not cite Vitruvius – the only authority he does cite in the chapter is Charles Perrault, the author of the *Parallèle des Anciens et Modernes* (1688) and the brother of Claude, the author of the work on columns[74] – he clearly aligns himself with Vitruvius's emphasis on the appearance of proportions to actual human observers as the real basis of beauty rather than with the purer rationalism of Alberti and Palladio. This is only to be expected from a writer so closely connected to the empiricist tradition in British philosophy. In fact, Kames emphasizes how things actually appear to us in the case of utility as well as beauty: "With respect to buildings of every sort, one rule, dictated by utility, is that they be firm and stable" (here is his passing reference to *firmitas*). "Another rule, dictated by beauty, is, that they also appear so: for what appears tottering and in hazard of tumbling, produceth in the spectator the painful emotion of fear, instead of the pleasant emotion of beauty; and, accordingly, it is the great care of the artist, that every part of his edifice appear to be well supported."[75] Here, though, Kames could be thinking of a remark by David Hume that "the rules of architecture require, that the top of a pillar shou'd be more slender than its base, and that because such a figure conveys to us the idea of security, which is pleasant; whereas the contrary form gives us the apprehension of danger, which is uneasy."[76] This concerns the effect of architecture upon our emotions more than on the physiology of perception – but then the central subject of Kames's *Elements of Criticism* is the emotional impact of art.

Nevertheless, most of his discussion of architectural beauty concerns what we actually perceive. Kames sees proportions in architecture as determined by both function and beauty. For example, "The proportions of a door are determined by the use to which it is destined. The door of a dwelling-house ... ought to correspond to the human size," while the "proportions proper for the door of a barn or a coach-house, are widely different." Further, "The size of windows ought to be proportioned to that of the room they illuminate," while "The steps of a stair ought to be accommodated to the human figure, without regarding any other proportion: they are accordingly the same in large and in small buildings."[77] But beauty has its own demands, and proportions among the dimensions of rooms, for example, may be governed by the requirements of beauty as well as of utility, or of beauty when they are not governed by utility. "The height of a room exceeding nine or ten feet, has little or no relation to utility; and therefore proportion is the only rule for determining a greater height."[78] Yet in a further comment on ceiling heights, Kames makes clear his view that in matters of proportion beauty lies in how they strike the eye, not pure mathematics. "That we are framed by nature to relish proportion as well as regularity," he says, "is indisputable; but that agreeable proportion should ... be confined to certain precise measures, is not warranted by experience," for an empiricist the ultimate arbiter of taste. For example, "In a sumptuous edifice, the capital rooms ought to be large .... But in things thus related, the mind requires not a precise or single proportion, rejecting all others; on the contrary, many different proportions are made equally welcome." This is especially true "With respect to the height of a room," where "the proportion it ought to bear to the length or the breadth, is arbitrary; and it cannot be otherwise, considering the uncertainty of the eye as to the height of a room, where it exceeds 17 or 18 feet."[79] The room just has to appear suitably high. This is a direct contradiction of Palladio's practice.

Kames similarly insists the pleasing proportions for each of the orders of columns are not precisely determined by mathematics but fall into a range. He adopts Albertian language in making the general claim that "Proportion of parts is not only itself a beauty; but is inseparably connected with a beauty of the highest relish, that of concord or harmony."[80] These terms seem to be Kames's translation of Alberti's term *concinnitas*, but he is returning to Vitruvius and differing from Alberti in insisting that what counts as such must be determined more by the eye than by mathematical reasoning.

Where Kames agrees with both Vitruvius and Alberti is in his emphasis on *decor* or propriety, but he gives this point his own flavor by connecting it to emotion. He calls this "the sense of congruity," and says that "every building [should] have an expression corresponding to its destination." His illustration of this thesis is shot through with terms for emotions:

> A palace ought to be sumptuous and grand; a private dwelling neat and modest; a play-house, gay and splendid; and a monument, gloomy and melancholy. . . . A Christian church is not considered to be a house for the Deity, but merely a place of worship: it ought therefore to be decent and plain, without much ornament: a situation ought to be chosen low and retired; because the congregation, during worship, ought to be humble, and disengaged from the world. Columns, beside their chief service of being supports, may contribute to that peculiar expression which the destination of a building requires: columns of different proportions, serve to express loftiness, lightness, &c. as well as strength.[81]

What Vitruvius had said about the choice of the order of columns being suitable to the deity a temple is intended to house, Kames puts in terms of the particular emotions different buildings are meant to arouse, or, as he terms it, express. His sense of what emotions a "Christian church" ought to express and by what means it should do so might be particularly Protestant or even Presbyterian, but the point is general.

Since Kames started by saying that true works of architecture aim at both functionality and aesthetic appeal, in his terms utility and beauty, his thought can only be that the expression of emotion contributes to the beauty of a building; he is not rejecting the Vitruvian categories, but expanding the meaning of one of them. The general scheme remains in force.

Laugier also demonstrates the continuing validity of the fundamental principles of Vitruvius. Laugier clearly wrote his *Essay on Architecture* under the influence of *The Fine Arts Reduced to a Single Principle*, published by his contemporary Charles Batteux (1713–80) in 1746.[82] Batteux's single principle was that beauty consists in the imitation of nature, although by imitation Batteux actually meant the idealization of nature: art should describe or present, depending on its medium, how nature ought to be rather than how it often actually is. Laugier took the idea of the imitation of nature more literally, and applied it to architecture through the idea of the primitive hut. He took this from Vitruvius but ignored Vitruvius's point that early humans in different environments would have developed different styles of building. Rather, starting from the premise that the earliest architecture would have consisted of houses built with four corner-posts connected by four crossing beams, on top of which a pitched roof would have been constructed to shed the rain, he inferred that the "general principles" of architecture are the column, the entablature (the horizontal beams resting on the columns), the pediment or gable ends (but only under the ends of the pitched roofs), windows and doors for access, egress, light and air, and in the fullness of time multiple stories.[83] His general principle is then that these structurally and functionally essential parts are "the cause of beauty," and thus that "If each of these parts is suitably placed and suitably formed, nothing else need be added to make the work perfect," while anything "added by caprice causes every fault."[84] His argument is therefore that beauty is essential to architecture, and that beauty lies in the imitation of nature, but that the relevant nature determines useful and possible structure, so that beauty arises from construction and function. Laugier writes in the terms of Batteux – "Let us keep to the simple and natural; it is the only road to beauty"[85] – but he cannot avoid the three general ideals of Vitruvius. His theory is just that beauty arises from useful construction. Laugier particularly objects to any sort of decoration – twisted rather than straight columns, pilasters, columns that do not sit on the ground like the original corner-posts of the hut but stand on their own pedestals, the paired columns in Perrault's facade for the Louvre – that does not serve a direct and original structural function. Laugier thus denies that there might be demands of beauty that are not also demands of utility. But beauty and utility can still be distinguished as two distinct ideals both to be realized through the third of good construction. His objection is just to attempting to achieve beauty through ornament with no useful or structural function.

Laugier's continuing commitment to the Vitruvian triad is evident in his Chapter III. Here he first takes up the topics of "solidity" and illustrates this with a few remarks about materials and construction;[86] second, "convenience," about which he says that "Buildings are made to be lived in and only as much as they are convenient can they be habitable," to which their "situation, planning, and internal communications" contribute;[87] and third, in the place of aesthetic appeal, what the translators leave untranslated as "*bienséance*." Presumably this could mean something like "good sense," and what is striking is that Laugier does not explicate it in formal terms, thus rejecting the Albertian interpretation of beauty or even the empiricist modification of the rationalist theory of proportion, but rather interprets it chiefly in terms of the category of *decor* or propriety. "*Bienséance* demands that a building is neither more nor less magnificent than is appropriate to its purpose, that is to say that the decoration of buildings should not be arbitrary, but must always be in relation to the rank and quality of those who live in them and conform to the objective envisaged."[88] This principle implies that the owners of private homes should not pretend by their buildings to be of higher rank than they really are, but it applies even to kings and princes, who should not build churches honoring themselves as if they were gods, and who might better use their pretentious churches as mausolea. But what is striking here is that even though Laugier, perhaps puritanically, militates against both a formalistic conception of beauty and the liberal use of ornament, he does so within the framework of the Vitruvian triad, just adapting the flexible category of aesthetic appeal for his own purposes.

Laugier does not take up Vitruvius's suggestion, in the form of his discussion of the Caryatids, that part of the aesthetic appeal of a building may be a conceptual meaning or a message. Against the more immediate background of thought from the Renaissance and the eighteenth century that we have just been considering, the emphasis on architectural meaning that we will now see to be prominent in the nineteenth and twentieth centuries might seem like a radical departure from the Vitruvian framework. In fact, it can be seen as the development of what was already an aspect of Vitruvius's own general concept of aesthetic appeal.

2   The Meaning of Beauty

From Kant to Semper

1 Kant

In the long century beginning with Immanuel Kant's third critique, the *Critique of the Power of Judgment*, published in 1790, the idea of meaning became central to the conception of the aesthetic appeal of architecture. A new idea also became important in thought about architecture in at least two ways: freedom of imagination became central to the understanding of the aesthetic appeal of architecture, and freedom in the creation and the use of architecture became central to the understanding of its functionality. The focus of this chapter will be the German philosophers Immanuel Kant (1724–1804) and his eccentric although influential follower Arthur Schopenhauer (1788–1860), the British artist and art critic as well as social theorist John Ruskin (1819–1900), and the German architect and architectural theorist Gottfried Semper (1803–79). Kant worked within the Vitruvian framework but expanded the concept of beauty to include at least two kinds of meaning, but Schopenhauer focused so narrowly on the meaning of architecture and its achievement through structure that he neglected the basic fact of its functionality. Ruskin also had little to say about utility, but his analysis of the multiple forms of meaning that can comprise beauty in architecture is so rich and also includes enough about the use of materials in architectural construction that he can be seen as enriching the Vitruvian categories of both construction and aesthetic appeal. Semper thought in terms of the basic functions and technologies of architecture rather than of meaning, but his analysis of how beauty arises from both the essential functions and the essential materials of architecture still tightly links the three original Vitruvian categories.

As a philosophy professor of modest means who never traveled far from remote Königsberg in East Prussia, Kant never saw any of the great monuments of European architecture. That he should have had anything to contribute to the development of thought about architecture might seem surprising. It might also seem surprising that he should be described as having accepted a Vitruvian conception of architecture while introducing an expanded conception of content or meaning into his treatment of architectural beauty. He is famous for the claims that judgments of taste are "disinterested": "if the question is whether something is beautiful, one does not want to know whether there is anything that is or that could be at stake, for us or for someone else, in the existence of the thing,"[1] and thus beauty is "entirely independent" from "objective purposiveness . . . i.e., the *utility* of the object."[2] There goes one of the Vitruvian ideals. Kant further claims that what seem to be paradigmatic cases of beauty, such as those of birds and shells, as well as designs *à la grecque*, foliage for borders and wallpapers, and fantasias or music without a text, "do not represent anything, no object under a determinate concept."[3] There goes, or so it would seem, any connection between beauty and meaning. However, Kant's view is not in fact that the kind of examples of beauty just cited, what he calls *free* beauties, are the most *important* kinds of beauty; they are just the *simplest* cases of beauty, from which aesthetic theory can set out in order to identify the key element in aesthetic experience and pleasure. Many cases of beauty, indeed perhaps the most numerous and most important, are what Kant calls *adherent* beauty, beauty that does presuppose a "concept of what the object ought to be," including the "particular end it ought to serve," and Kant illustrates this kind of beauty with architectural examples: churches, palaces, arsenals, and garden-houses.[4] Further, when he comes to talk specifically about the fine or "beautiful arts" (*schöne Künste*), Kant says that "Beauty (whether it be beauty of nature or of art) can in general be called the expression of aesthetic ideas," as we will see, a special kind of content. He bases a whole scheme for the classification of the arts, explicitly including architecture, on this thesis. In the case of architecture, then, its beauty will include content, and its beauty will coexist with utility. Like other philosophers, Kant has nothing much to say about good construction, but he assumes that it is through good construction that the twin ideals of functionality and beauty including meaning will be achieved.

Kant's first great work, the *Critique of Pure Reason* (1781), had concerned the nature of knowledge and the mental faculties of sensibility and understanding on which it rests as well as its limits; the *Critique of Practical Reason* (1788) concerned the fundamental principle of morality as well as the freedom of the will that makes it at least possible for us to act in accordance with this principle.[5] Kant's "Critique of the Aesthetic Power of Judgment," the first half of the *Critique of the Power of Judgment* (1790),[6] begins from an analysis of judgments of taste, what we now call aesthetic judgments. Kant argues that judgments of beauty (and subsequently the more complex judgments of the sublime) must be both about and made on the basis of the pleasure that one actually feels in response to the representation of an object, whether in perception or in imagination, and so are in one sense about one's response to an object rather than about the object itself.[7] However, such judgments can take the verbal form of predicating a property, beauty (or sublimity), of their object,[8] because they speak with a "universal voice," that is, they claim to be valid for anyone who approaches the object in the right circumstances and frame of mind, like other kinds of judgments. Kant's philosophical challenge is then to explain how the representation of an object can produce a feeling of pleasure that is not just a personal, idiosyncratic response, like my preference for German Riesling over Californian Chardonnay, but a response that is interpersonally valid, at least under ideal conditions. His answer to this puzzle is that our underlying response to a beautiful object cannot be simply a matter of classifying an object under a determinate concept, like calling something a bicycle because it has two wheels, because that is a mechanical process that does not produce any noticeable pleasure once the concept has been learned;[9] yet our response must nevertheless involve our cognitive powers, specifically our powers of both understanding and imagination, which can be presumed to work pretty much the same way in everyone.[10] Kant's proposal is that if these mental abilities are not to function in their normal, basically boring way of subsuming objects under concepts (as in "That's an Ionic column because it has the Ionic capital"), then the relation between them must be the one that he characterizes with the metaphor of "free play" or "mutual animation." Kant's basic idea is that we find an object pleasing and beautiful when the experience that it affords us – the "manifold," of shapes, sounds, visual images, and ultimately symbols of ideas – *feels* coherent and unified to us to even though its coherence does *not* follow from any obvious concept or rule (like "An Ionic column must have these features . . ."). Beauty is a pleasant surprise. Kant suggests this theory in a number of passages, such as this one from the Introduction to his book,

> [If] the imagination . . . is unintentionally brought into accord with the understanding . . . through a given representation and a feeling of pleasure is thereby aroused, then the object must be regarded as purposive for the [aesthetic] power of judgment. Such a judgment is an aesthetic judgment on the purposiveness of the object, which is not grounded on any available concept of the object and does not furnish one.

Kant's view of beauty is a version of the traditional theory that it consists in unity amidst variety, with the clarification that the unity cannot be concept-dependent or rule-driven. Yet Kant initially restricts the object of beauty solely to the form of objects. Thus he continues:

> That object the form of which (not the material aspect of its representation, as sensation) in mere reflection on

> it . . . is judged as the ground of a pleasure in the
> representation of such an object – with its representation
> this pleasure is also judged to be necessarily combined,
> consequently not merely for the subject who apprehends
> this form but for everyone who judges at all. The object is
> then called beautiful . . ."[11]

By "form" in such a remark Kant seems to mean only spatial and/or temporal form as contrasted to sensory qualities of objects such as color or timbre, thus "drawing" (*Zeichnung*) or design rather than color in the case of "all the pictorial arts" and "architecture and horticulture insofar as they are fine arts" and "composition" rather than "the agreeable tones of instruments" in the case of music.[12] This would seem to be a serious restriction in the case of architecture, not to speak of painting, and part of Kant's omission of the role of materials in architecture and indeed anything much to do with actual construction. Kant's basic idea, then, is that in the experience of beauty we have a feeling of unity or coherence that is independent from a concept, or, more precisely, since we do apply *some* concepts to everything that we experience, that goes beyond that unity dictated by any concept that we do apply – a beautiful bird, for example a hummingbird rather than a crow, is one that just as much as the other satisfies the criteria for being a bird, but seems to us to have a graceful, elegant, unified form (and coloration, anyone other than Kant would add) that goes beyond merely satisfying those criteria. However, this turns out to be more flexible than it first appears, and makes room for a complex conception of architectural beauty and the relation of such beauty to utility.[13]

In this analysis Kant has been focused on the experience of the *observer* of a beautiful object or the *audience* for it, should it be a work of art, rather than anything about the *producer* of the object or the *artist*. Friedrich Nietzsche famously criticized Kant on just this point,[14] but in fact Kant has a complementary theory of the artist, his theory of "genius." This comes later in his book, as the core of his theory of beautiful art as opposed to beauty in general, and it is there that Kant suddenly asserts that the expression of "aesthetic ideas" is essential to beauty. But first Kant expands his initial analysis of beauty to the case in which beauty is compatible with rather than contrasted to utility. Free beauties, as Kant now designates the kind of beauty he has been discussing thus far, presuppose no concept of "what the object ought to be," adherent beauties do. Examples of free beauty are the beauty of flowers, shells, birds, and the decorative arts and music without words; cases of adherent beauty include the beauty of "a human being (and in this species that of a man, a woman, or a child), the beauty of a horse, [and] of a building (such as a church, a palace, an arsenal, or a garden-house)."[15] Coming after Kant's previous claims that beauty has nothing to do with the subsumption of an object under a concept, that Kant should now recognize adherent beauty as a kind of beauty at all may seem surprising. But Kant's theory of free play resolves the apparent contradiction: after all, we subsume *every* object of our attention under some concept or other – we have to recognize the flower *as* a flower in order to say "This flower is beautiful" – so the room for the free play of the imagination within the confines of the understanding's general demand for unity must lie in the space that is not determined by the concept. We use the concept *flower* to identify the object we are attending to and talking about, but what it takes to satisfy the concept is not what makes the flower beautiful, for there are plain or downright ugly flowers too. Kant does not unpack his examples of adherent beauty, but we can apply a similar analysis, with one variation: in these cases, the conditions for satisfying the concept involved are *necessary* conditions for our finding the object beautiful. However, they are still not *sufficient* conditions: there must still be free play of the imagination within the limits set for us by those conditions for us to find the object beautiful.

Take Kant's architectural examples: each of them implies necessary but not sufficient conditions for beauty for that kind of building. Thus, a church may have to have a cruciform floor-plan, a palace grand reception rooms, an arsenal thick walls, and a garden-house a broad roof to provide shade from the sun and shelter from a sudden shower but open walls to admit pleasant breezes; but of course there can be aesthetically indifferent or downright ugly churches, palaces, arsenals, and garden-houses that nevertheless satisfy these requirements. The program – the intended function – of these building types places certain necessary conditions on their overall design, but these are not sufficient conditions for designing beautiful buildings. It may be a matter of human psychology that we cannot find buildings beautiful if they obviously fail at their intended function, but beauty will always require more than what is directly determined by the requirements of any specific intended function. From Kant's point of view, function never fully determines form; imagination must always be added. Merely satisfying the functional requirements of its program is not sufficient to make a building beautiful. When a church is beautiful, its beauty must be compatible with the required floor-plan and such other constraints as the orientation of its entrance and the location of its pulpit, but must consist in more: formal features not determined by the program, materials, decoration, in short, everything that might be the product of the free play of imagination in the architect and contribute to free play of the imagination in the audience. Aesthetic appeal cannot conflict with functionality, but is not produced simply by functionality.

A stronger claim would be that the beauty of an object that has a definite purpose should not merely be compatible with that function but should be in some way harmonious with or even expressive of it. Kant does not explicitly say this, but neither does he exclude it, and indeed when he returns to the case of architecture in his sketch of a system of the arts he may come close to saying it. So now let's turn to Kant's theory of art.[16]

Kant defines art in general as "production through freedom" or intentional human production that requires skill as opposed to technical knowledge alone; beautiful or fine art (*schöne Kunst*), which includes architecture, is art aimed at the production of pleasure in beauty, although such art also requires some technical rules, or "a *mechanism*, without which the *spirit*, which must be *free* in the art and which alone animates the work, would have no body at all and would entirely evaporate."[17] As we have already seen, in the case of adherent beauty the goal of aesthetic appeal is also at least compatible with that of functionality. Having just stated that art is the product of human intention and having earlier argued that the beauty of art, specifically of architecture, is compatible with functionality, Kant then makes another apparently paradoxical assertion: "In a product of art one must be aware that it is art, and not nature; yet the purposiveness in its form must still seem to be as free from all constraint by arbitrary rules as if it were a mere product of nature."[18] However, this paradox is resolved by Kant's conception of genius as the source of art: In genius, "the gift of nature must give the rule to art (as beautiful art),"[19] that is, in the production of successful art, nature works *through* the artist. Less metaphorically, in the production of beauty the artist's imagination goes beyond the specific intentions of the artist, for example an architectural program, and also goes beyond the technical rules that the artist must follow in her specific medium, for example, rules of the constructional methods or technology employed. Whatever specific intentions the artist may have and whatever technical rules the artist may need to follow – the rules of single vanishing point perspective, the rule to put fast-drying paint under slow-drying paint but not vice versa, the rules for designing a column in one order or another or for determining the pitch of a roof necessary at a certain location – the artist needs *freedom* of imagination to produce something beautiful.

However, if we now recall Kant's original explanation of *anyone's* pleasure in beauty, we will realize that the freedom of the imagination of *artists* must both leave room for and stimulate free play of the imagination on the part of their *audiences* as well as for themselves. Kant models this relation of freedom in one stimulating freedom in the other in the case of relations among artists: "genius is the exemplary originality of the natural endowment of a subject for the *free* use of his cognitive faculties," but that use of freedom must be a model "for emulation by another genius, who is thereby awakened to the feeling of his own originality."[20] This must be so in the relation of one artist to another; think of Beethoven as the student of Haydn, or of Frank Lloyd Wright as the student of Louis Sullivan, himself the student of H. H. Richardson. But it also applies to the relation of artist to audience – without free play on the part of whoever is to appreciate beauty as well as create it, there can be no pleasure in it. This is one constraint on any art, including architecture: the freedom of imagination on the part of the artist must be compatible with as well as a stimulus to the freedom of imagination on the part of the audience. Some architects might be geniuses, but they cannot design merely to please themselves. This is a practical point, of course – they usually build with other people's money – but in Kant's view it is also a requirement of the logic of taste.

Kant further claims that the "spirit" of all beautiful art consists in "the presentation of *aesthetic ideas*," representations of the imagination that occasion "much thinking though without it being possible for any determinate thought, i.e., *concept*, to be adequate to it, which, consequently, no language fully attains or can make intelligible." Here Kant is adding that artistic beauty involves the free play of the imagination *with ideas or content as well as with pure form.* Kant illustrates his theory with the example of morally significant ideas: "The poet ventures to make sensible rational ideas of invisible beings, the kingdom of the blessed, the kingdom of hell, eternity, creation, etc."[21] He does not explain why the content of art should be limited to *moral* ideas, although several pages later he asserts that only moral ideas can sufficiently sustain our interest to prevent the mind becoming "aware that its disposition is contrapurposive in the judgment of reason," and therefore "dissatisfied with itself and moody."[22] His thought now seems to be that we can take pleasure in mere form for a while, but in the end that will "serve only for diversion" and will pale if it is not connected with the expression of some morally significant idea about the human condition. This requirement would apply to architecture along with the other fine arts.

Kant may seem to go too far when he suggests that *all* successful works of art, including works of architecture, must express some moral idea, and he certainly seems to go too far when he asserts that all "Beauty (whether it be beauty of nature or of art) can in general be called the *expression* of aesthetic ideas."[23] But certainly some works of architecture can express ideas, as a Gothic or Counter-Reformation Baroque cathedral may express certain Christian conceptions of the deity or a Buddhist stupa or Shinto shrine may express very different religious ideas, or even as when the Caryatids of the Erechtheum expressed the Athenians' contempt for the Carians. We could certainly debate whether this is a valid requirement of all architecture. Be that as it may, Kant suggests a further kind of architectural meaning when he presents his system of the arts. Here, finally, is what Kant has specifically to say about architecture:

> The plastic arts [*Plastik*], as the first kind of beautiful visual [*bildender*] arts, include *sculpture* and *architecture*. The *first* is that which presents corporeal concepts of things as they *could* exist in nature (although, as a beautiful art, with regard to aesthetic purposiveness); the *second* is the art of presenting, with this intention but yet at the same time in an aesthetically purposive way, concepts of things that are possible *only through art*, and whose form has as its determining ground not nature but a voluntary end. In the latter a certain *use* of the artistic object is the main thing, to which, as a condition, the aesthetic ideas are restricted. In the former the mere *expression* of aesthetic ideas is the chief aim. The statues of humans, gods, animals, etc., are of the first sort; but temples, magnificent buildings for public gatherings, as well as dwellings, triumphal arches, cenotaphs, and the like, erected as memorials, belong to architecture. Indeed, all domestic furnishings (the work of the carpenter and the like things for use) can be counted as belonging to the latter, because the appropriateness of the product to a certain use is essential in a *work of architecture*, while by contrast a mere *picture*, which is made strictly for viewing and is to please for itself, is, as a corporeal presentation, a mere imitation of nature, although with respect to aesthetic ideas: where, then, *sensible truth* should not go so far that it stops looking like art and a product of the power of choice.[24]

There is a great deal going on in this passage. Kant is thinking of sculpture as the imitation of natural objects – obviously he was not familiar with the abstract sculpture of

Alexander Calder or Richard Serra – that has no other purpose or function in mind than formal beauty as well as the expression of some aesthetic ideas. This may not seem quite right, since sculpture can often be made to serve some religious, civic, or political goal. Kant's line between sculpture and architecture may also seem fuzzy, because some of the genres that he mentions as examples of architecture, such as triumphal arches and cenotaphs, may not have much function beyond the memorial or celebratory functions that sculpture can have. Nevertheless, the main cases of architecture clearly realize multiple ends: they must serve some specific purpose, and serve it well, such as that of a dwelling, a temple, a public building; they must be beautiful, although within the confines of "the appropriateness of the product to a certain use," which in architecture is "essential" or the main thing; and they must express some aesthetic idea or ideas. Some of Kant's examples confirm his previous claim that aesthetic ideas must express morally significant ideas: a temple can express an idea of divinity, a public building an idea of justice, a triumphal arch the idea of a well-governed state, perhaps even a dwelling the idea of the institutions of marriage and family. Sometimes this will be assisted by a sculptural program, as when a Greek temple contains the statue of its dedicatee in addition to employing the relevant order for the god or goddess being honored, or when the west front of a cathedral has an elaborate sculptural program; sometimes an inscription may help, in which case the boundaries between supposedly distinct arts – architecture on the one hand and poetry or oratory on the other – will be crossed; sometimes the idea will be expressed by more purely architectural means – by the floor-plan of a building, by its size, its site, and so on. In any case, there can be no exact rule for how a building should express an aesthetic idea, because then there would be no beauty in that expression, or the expression would not be aesthetic.

But now comes the further suggestion. Kant's remark that architecture is "the art of presenting [*darzustellen*], with this intention but yet in an aesthetically purposive way, concepts of things that are possible only through art" might mean merely that works of architecture *realize* or *instantiate* conceptions of human purposes or uses rather than imitating natural objects. Depending on how the term "presenting" is understood, however, Kant might also mean that works of architecture should present *themselves*, or make clear the kind of function that they do have – that a house should *look like* a house, not a factory or a temple, that a temple should look like a temple, not a house or a factory, and so on. This may be a stretch, and in any case would have to take account that ideas about what a house or a temple or another building type should look like will vary widely from one culture, time, and/or place to another, so such a requirement would have to be applied contextually. Nevertheless, Kant might here be anticipating one interpretation of the later slogan "form follows function": the intended function of a structure should constrain certain features of its design – a house must have a kitchen and one or more bathrooms, a temple or triumphal arch need not – but should also determine something about how the structure looks – although in neither case could or should the intended function determine everything about design and appearance, because then there will be no room for beauty.

So, although he had nothing special to say about good construction, Kant clearly worked with the Vitruvian categories of functionality and aesthetic appeal and recognized the complex relations between them. He treated functionality as a necessary condition in the case of architecture as an art of adherent rather than free beauty, but also expanded the conception of architecture's aesthetic appeal in two ways. First, Kant analyzed the experience of beauty in terms of freedom of the imagination; he left that largely as a philosophical metaphor, but can be taken to have given his blessing for the subsequent development of the Romantic conception of the artist, although with the proviso that the artist's freedom must stimulate the freedom of the audience, not dominate it. Second, Kant included in his conception of the aesthetic appeal or "spirit" of art the expression of content as aesthetic ideas, which may include the abstract ideas of morality (for Kant religion is only the symbolic expression of morality) but also of building types themselves. But before we move on, one last point about Kant.

So far I have stressed his view that beauty lies in the freedom of the *imagination*, whatever exactly that is, but that artistic success requires room for the freedom of imagination in both artist and audience. But Kant also holds that *every* human action must be governed by morality, and what morality requires, in the simplest terms, is that in every human interaction each person involved must be treated as an end and not merely as a means, or that each person must be as free to set her own ends as is compatible with everyone else involved doing the same. The guiding thought of Kantian morality is the *maximal equal freedom* of all human beings – that every human being must be as free as is possible compatibly with the equal freedom of every other. This is the message of Kant's "formula of humanity" in his *Groundwork for the Metaphysics of Morals* (1785), and of his "Universal Principle of Right" in his *Metaphysics of Morals* (1797), that "Any action is *right* if it can coexist with everyone's freedom in accordance with a universal law, or if on its maxim the freedom of choice of each can coexist with everyone's freedom."[25] This general principle applies to the interaction between artists and their audiences too, thus in the case of architecture to the interaction between architects and their clients, other users of their buildings, even to broader publics: the freedom of architects to design what and as they please is not complete and cannot come at any and all cost to the audience for their work, but must be reconciled with the freedom of the audience. Perhaps there can be such a thing as complete poetic license in poetry – no one has to buy a book of poetry, and even if they do it does not cost very much – but something as complex and costly as architecture, a business as well as an art, is another matter. The freedom of all involved must be equally respected.

The "German idealist" philosophers who followed Kant, especially the first-generation figures Friedrich Wilhelm Joseph Schelling (1775–1854), Friedrich Wilhelm Hegel (1770–1831), and Arthur Schopenhauer, as well as second-generation figures, chief among them Friedrich Theodor Vischer (1807–87), developed elaborate systems of the arts grounded on Kant's claim that the spirit of fine art consists in the expression of aesthetic ideas. In some cases, such as that of Hegel, they focused on the intellectual content of art to the exclusion of everything else, leading to the neglect of the Vitruvian values of good construction and functionality in the case of architecture, or even the rejection of functionality as an important consideration altogether. There is no space here to discuss these elaborate systems, but let's pause briefly over Schopenhauer, whose suppression of the importance of programmatic function in architecture is combined with a striking emphasis on the expression of ideas through structural function, and who for that reason anticipates, although from his peculiar philosophical point of view, a major thread of later architectural thought.[26]

2 Schopenhauer

Schopenhauer adopted Kant's "transcendental idealism," the view that the spatiotemporal and causal structure of the world is only the way in which we *represent* the reality that underlies both ourselves and all the other objects we experience, or the way the world *appears*. But while Kant had argued that the gap between appearance and reality leaves room for the possibility that our own wills may be completely free to act in accordance with pure (moral) reason in a way that we do not always, or almost ever, observe at the level of appearance, Schopenhauer supposed that underlying all appearance is a single, non-rational will, insatiable and never satisfied – thus the title of his *magnum opus*, *The World as Will and Representation*

(1819, expanded second edition 1844). At the human level, he took this to mean that individuals are all driven by insatiable desires, which doom us all to perpetual dissatisfaction: either desire is not satisfied at all, or it is satisfied but we soon become satiated and bored – either way, we end up unhappy. This is the reason why the practical functions of architectural works are of no interest to Schopenhauer. The only long-term solution to this unhappy fate, he argued, is complete abnegation of self-interest, replacing self-concern with compassion for the suffering of all sentient beings, which are at bottom one. But *beauty*, specifically the beauty of art, including architecture, offers at least short-term relief from perpetual frustration. It does this, Schopenhauer argues, by presenting the essences of reality at different levels, ranging from the most elementary forces of nature to human actions rather than individual things, with all their never-satisfying connections to our individual desires: contemplation of these essences, or "Platonic Ideas" as he calls them, as presented by works of art, offers us at least temporary relief from the cycle of individual desire and frustration that otherwise ends only with death. In the contemplation of the general ideas presented by art,

> pure knowing comes to us, so to speak, in order to deliver us from willing and its stress. We follow, yet only for a few moments; willing, desire, the recollection of our own personal aims, always tears us anew from peaceful contemplation; but yet again and again, the next beautiful environment, in which pure, will-less knowledge presents itself to us, entices us away from willing.[27]

Schopenhauer's idea that art offers relief from frustrated desire is his reinterpretation of Kant's notion of the disinterested pleasure of beauty in the representation rather than actual existence of objects, and his notion that it does this through the contemplation of Platonic Ideas is his reinterpretation of Kant's notion of aesthetic ideas, although for Schopenhauer these ideas concern all levels of appearance rather than moral ideas only.

There are two chief implications of Schopenhauer's theory for the case of architecture. First, since the attempt to find pleasure in the satisfaction of particular needs or desires is hopeless, in an explicit departure from the Vitruvian paradigm Schopenhauer severs genuine architecture altogether from considerations of utility. Thus "if we consider *architecture* merely as a fine art and apart from its provision for useful purposes, in which it serves the will and not pure knowledge, and is thus no longer art in our sense, we can assign it no purpose other than that of bringing to clearer perceptiveness some of those Ideas" the contemplation of which brings the sought-after if only temporary relief from the frustration of desire.[28] Second, the Ideas that architecture is supposed to present are those of the most elementary forces of nature, namely "gravity, cohesion, rigidity, fluidity, light, and so on . . . . [T]hose universal qualities of stone, those, first, simplest, and dullest visibilities of the will." In addition to calling these Ideas "dullest," Schopenhauer also characterizes the forces of nature they represent as the "lowest" and "weakest," which seems counterintuitive; as the most fundamental forces of nature, they might also be thought to be the most ubiquitous and strongest – after all, what can violate the law of gravity? Be that as it may, Schopenhauer draws the conclusion that "the conflict between gravity and rigidity is the sole aesthetic material of architecture," and that "its problem is to make this conflict appear with perfect distinctiveness" so that we can contemplate it.

> Therefore the beauty of a building is certainly to be found in the evident and obvious suitability of every part, not to the outward arbitrary purpose of man (to this extent the work belongs to practical architecture), but directly to the stability of the whole. The position, size, and form of every part must have so necessary a relation to this stability that if it were possible to remove some part, the whole would inevitably collapse. For only by each part bearing as much as it conveniently can, and each being supported exactly where it ought to be and to exactly the necessary extent, does this play of opposites, this conflict between rigidity and gravity, that constitutes the life of the stone and the manifestation of its will, unfold itself in the most complete visibility.[29]

This statement revises Alberti's definition of beauty, as that which is diminished by the removal of any part, into purely structural terms. It is as pure a statement of structural functionalism as can be found: the beauty of architecture lies solely in the expression of the function of its materials and the type of structure they necessitate. In particular, for Schopenhauer the purest form of architecture is rigid columns resisting the weight of the beams that sit upon them. The "sole and constant theme" of architecture is "*support* and *load*," and the "purest execution of this theme is column and entablature; hence the order of columns has become the thorough-base of the whole of architecture."[30] Schopenhauer uses his metaphysics to justify the focus on the classical orders from Vitruvius through Alberti, Palladio, and the Perraults – and their continuing use in his own time. He concludes that because the essence of architecture is fully realized in the expression of the forces of gravity and rigidity in the resistance of columns to their load, architecture was "perfect and complete in essential matters" since antiquity, and "has no longer been capable of any important enrichment." So "the modern architect cannot noticeably depart from the rules and models of the ancients, without being on the path of degeneration. Therefore there is nothing left for him to do but to apply the art handed down by the ancients."[31] In particular, Schopenhauer uses his philosophical theory to reject the Gothic revival that was well on its way at least by his second edition of 1844. "Perhaps a certain beauty is not to be totally denied" to the "so-called Gothic style, which is of Saracen origin, and was introduced to the rest of Europe by the Goths in Spain," but for this style "to undertake to set itself up, however, as the equal in status of the ancient style, is a barbarous presumption that must not for one moment be allowed."[32] Schopenhauer protests against the incipient historicism of later nineteenth–century architecture: no historical style except the classical expresses the essential forces of nature, which is the sole source of beauty in architecture.

Schopenhauer also draws more particular conclusions from his metaphysically based structural functionalism. In one passage, with examples that must come from

Laugier, he rejects any form of columns that goes beyond structural necessity: "the form of each part must be determined not arbitrarily, but by its purpose and relation to the whole. The column is the simplest form of support, determined merely by the purpose or intention." Thus "The twisted column is tasteless; the four-corned pillar is in fact less simple than the round column, though it happens to be more easily made," which for Schopenhauer is an irrelevant matter of economy, thus of utility.[33] Schopenhauer also objected to the peaked roofs of northern Europe as contrasted to the "very flat" roofs of Italy on the grounds that they contribute nothing to, even detract from, the clear expression of the relation of support to load:

> A high roof is neither support nor load, for its two halves mutually support each other, but the whole has no weight corresponding to its extension. It therefore presents to the eye an extended mass; this is wholly foreign to the aesthetic end, serves a merely useful purpose, and consequently disturbs the aesthetic, the theme of which is always support and load alone.[34]

Schopenhauer rejects steeply pitched roofs in spite of their evident utility in shedding rain and snow because they do not clearly express the fundamental forces of gravity and rigidity. He does not seem to consider that even the architects of the Greek temples that are his model of architectural beauty must also have considered this aspect of utility, because they crowned their entablatures with tiled peaked roofs over timber frames, although with less rain and rare snow they could use a lower pitch for their roofs than would be useful further north. Actual Greek architecture considered multiple factors of utility in conjunction with solidity and beauty; Schopenhauer's argument for Greek Revival does not. It would no doubt give Schopenhauer too much influence to suggest that his philosophical argument was the source of the preference for flat roofs in twentieth-century modernist architecture no matter what the local climatic conditions might be, but his disregard for considerations of utility and ultimately perhaps structural integrity (because flat roofs so readily leak and damage the rest of a structure) was shared by much later architecture.[35]

While he rejected all considerations of utility in favor of an account of architectural beauty as an expression of the most basic structural forms, Schopenhauer nevertheless closely linked the two Vitruvian categories of construction and beauty. Let us now turn from Germany to Britain to look at another theorist who also played down utility while insisting on the truthful expression of structure, but also vastly expanded his conception of the aesthetic appeal of architecture to include many dimensions of meaning. I refer to John Ruskin.

3 Ruskin

Ruskin was trained neither as a philosopher nor as an architect. If he was trained to be anything at all, he trained himself to be a geologist. But he became an accomplished artist (he illustrated his books on architecture with his own sketches), the leading art critic of Victorian Britain, and ultimately a powerful social critic and moralist as well.

He wrote voluminously: his complete works run to thirty-nine volumes.[36] He first made his mark with a volume on *Modern Painters*, published when he was only twenty-four, in defense of the painter J. M. W. Turner (1775–1851) – there were ultimately five volumes under this title. His chief works on architecture were *The Seven Lamps of Architecture*, published in 1849, and then *The Stones of Venice*, three volumes published from 1851 to 1853. Even though he was not a philosopher, Ruskin cannot be omitted from a history of philosophical aesthetics, because he assimilated so much of previous philosophical aesthetics and had a large influence on aesthetics into the twentieth century; likewise he cannot be omitted from even a brief history of architectural thought because of the intrinsic interest of his ideas and his influence on the practice of architecture, at least in Britain and the US, for several decades.[37]

Ruskin was an only child brought up near London by Scottish parents who were both wealthy and devout Protestants, particularly his mother. His thought was thoroughly imbued with the Bible, and his term "lamps" in the title *The Seven Lamps of Architecture* comes from a line in Psalm 119, "Thy Word is a lamp unto my feet." By the "lamps" of architecture Ruskin means "those large principles of right which are applicable to every stage and style" of architecture, which he describes as itself "uniting the technical and imaginative elements as essentially as humanity does soul and body."[38] Ruskin's word "principles" is a better choice than the word "laws" he uses later on the same page, when he says that there are general laws not "peculiar to any one art" but which "have modified forms and operations belonging to each," because he does not have in mind determinate rules that can be mechanically applied; what he has in mind by "lamps" can best be described as general values or sources of pleasure that may be realized in architecture, although exactly which should be realized in any particular work and how will always be a matter of context and judgment. We can call Ruskin's "lamps" principles as long as we do not take that to mean that they function as rules. The description of architecture as an art "uniting the technical and imaginative" is also significant: it reveals that Ruskin's primary interest is in construction on the one hand and beauty on the other. His seven principles constitute an expansive conception of architectural beauty, although several also bear on the character and quality of the materials and structural technologies of architecture.

The seven principles are sacrifice, truth, power, beauty, life, memory, and obedience. None of these have an immediate connection with utility, and it might seem that only what Ruskin calls beauty proper promises a direct connection with the kinds of formal qualities – eurythmy, symmetry, and so on – that were foregrounded in Vitruvius's original definition of *venustas*. However, although he does state that "Architecture concerns itself only with those characters of an edifice which are above and beyond its common use," this is not to say that Ruskin rejects utility as antipathetic to genuine architecture, as Schopenhauer had. Rather, he says that he confines "the name to that art which, taking up and admitting as conditions of its working, the necessities and common uses of the building, impresses on its form certain characters venerable or beautiful, but otherwise unnecessary."[39] This suggests that successfully satisfying some intended function is a *necessary* condition of architectural success, but that architectural beauty lies in ways in which buildings transcend ordinary functionality and the principles of architecture primarily concern its aesthetic appeal. In this way Ruskin's conception of architectural beauty could be taken to illustrate and expand Kant's category of adherent beauty. But Ruskin might also suggest an expansion of the conception of architectural functionality when he states that "Architecture is the art which so disposes and adorns the edifices raised by man, for whatsoever uses, that the sight of them may contribute to his mental health, power, and pleasure."[40] This suggests that architecture can positively contribute to our mental health and power, to our well-being, and surely that is as genuine a form of utility as providing a dry place to sleep or secure storage for grains or arms. Ruskin also reveals that he is not completely excluding considerations of utility from architecture when he states that

> Architecture, proper, then, naturally arranges itself under five heads:–
>
> Devotional; including all buildings raised for God's service or honour.
> Memorial; including both monuments and tombs.
> Civil; including every edifice raised by nations or societies, for purposes of common business or pleasure.
> Military; including all private and public architecture of defense.
> Domestic; including every rank and kind of dwelling-place.[41]

The main branches of architecture are thus defined by nothing other than the intended uses of buildings, in the most ordinary sense of use – for worship, for commemoration, for all kinds of public and private business, for defense, and for housing. So in the end Ruskin refines but hardly rejects the Vitruvian framework. However, his exposition is not organized as a theory of building types, as are the texts of Vitruvius, Alberti, or Palladio. Rather, while he acknowledges different uses of buildings and therefore different building types, Ruskin is interested in sources of well-being and pleasure not directly correlated to building type.

Some of Ruskin's principles describe ways in which people can make statements by their buildings, although not always statements that could be neatly expressed in words. The lamp of sacrifice, to begin, "prompts us to the offering of precious things, merely because they are precious, not because they are useful or necessary"[42] – that is, it consists in the use of expensive materials, for example, marbles and gilding, expensive techniques, such as elaborate tracery, perhaps the generous use of space itself, in ways beyond what is necessary for a building to fulfill its basic intended function. The point of this principle is to "exercise self-denial for the sake of self-discipline merely," in order to express "the desire to honour or please someone else by the costliness of the sacrifice."[43] That is, lavish, not strictly necessary spending on a church or a courthouse can express devotion to God or justice because it comes at the cost of spending on other things. The lamp of sacrifice may be more relevant to devotional, memorial, or civil architecture than to military or domestic building, for example, and Ruskin never says that each building type must exploit each principle. But other kinds of buildings might also make statements: a military structure can convey a threat or a boast of resistance, for example, although probably not by the use of lavish materials, while the statement that a private house might make by its lavishness could be offensive, the very opposite of self-sacrifice.

What sorts of values a building should express or what statements it should make is a deeply moral matter for Ruskin. This is obvious in the case of the lamp of truth, perhaps the most influential of Ruskin's principles. It is defined in negative terms as the necessity of avoiding "pretence, concealment, and deceit" in architecture: these are moral failings, so in architecture "a direct falsity of assertion respecting the nature of material, or the quantity of labour," is "contemptible," a failure of "conscience."[44] It is in his illustration of the principle of truth that Ruskin deals most directly with matters of materials and structure:

> Architectural Deceits are broadly to be considered under three heads:–
>
> 1st. The suggestion of a mode of structure or support other than the true one; as in pendants of late Gothic roofs.
> 2nd. The painting of surfaces to represent some other material than that of which they actually consist (as in the marbling of wood), or the deceptive representation of sculptured ornament upon them.
> 3rd. The use of cast or machine-made ornaments of any kind.[45]

Ruskin's antipathy to the machine-made is a central theme in *The Stones of Venice*. We will come back to that. His idea in the first two points is not that devices masking the underlying structure may not be pretty, interesting, elegant, in a word beautiful or pleasing on aesthetic grounds alone. Pendants or, in another of his examples, fan-vaulting that is not structurally necessary, may well be, and marbling might be as pretty as marble. Perhaps the lavish fan-vaulting of King's College Chapel, Cambridge, should even be approved under the principle of sacrifice. But Ruskin's present point is that deceit is morally objectionable, and if we become aware of it, as we inevitably do, it will interfere with whatever other pleasure we might take in an object. And unlike spending extra money on structurally unnecessary fan-vaulting, using a cheaper method to mimic a more expensive material, like marbling instead of marble, could not satisfy the lamp of sacrifice. Not every building must satisfy every principle, but no principle can be violated by any building if we are to find it appealing.

Ruskin's first point about truth is that deceit is morally objectionable, and this blocks other possible pleasures. He also suggests that there is a positive pleasure in the intelligibility of structure. Thus "so long as we see the stones and joints, and are not deceived as to the point of support in any piece of object, we may rather praise than regret the dextrous artifices which compel us to feel as if there were fibre in its shafts and life in its branches." Further, "the moment that the conditions of weight are comprehended, both truth and feeling require that the conditions of support should also be comprehended."[46]

Architectural truth is complex: deceit is intrinsically unpleasant, while being able to comprehend the structure of a work and the real contribution of its materials to that structure is intrinsically pleasant. With the second half of this position Ruskin anticipates later conceptions of structural functionalism, the thought that beauty lies directly in the clear expression of structure. But the lamp of truth is only one of seven, so Ruskin never suggests that this is the exclusive source of architectural beauty.

In the course of his exposition of architectural truth Ruskin makes one of the most notorious remarks in *The Seven Lamps*:

> [architecture] having been, up to the beginning of the [nineteenth] century, practised for the most part in clay, stone, or wood, it has resulted that the sense of proportion and the laws of structure have been based, the one altogether, the other in great part, on the necessities consequent on the employment of those materials; and that the entire or principle employment of metallic framework would, therefore, be generally felt as a departure from the first principles of art.

This seems to be the conservative trying to stop progress, exemplified by the structural use of iron, then glass and steel, in construction. However, Ruskin immediately modulates his assertion: "Abstractedly there appears no reason why iron should not be used as well as wood; and the time is probably near when a new system of architectural laws will be developed, adapted almost entirely to metallic construction."[47] What he is saying is that aesthetic preferences are not the responses of ahistorical subjects to contextless objects, but the responses of historically situated subjects to objects that have their own history. Change in aesthetic preferences is possible, indeed perhaps inevitable, but is not to be expected overnight.

The role of history in our experience of architecture is the explicit subject of Ruskin's sixth lamp, memory. But before that there come power, beauty, and life. The lamps of beauty and power are Ruskin's version of the eighteenth-century dichotomy of the beautiful and sublime. Ruskin's conception of power in architecture is closer to Kant's conception of the sublime than to that of Edmund Burke:[48] while for Burke the sublime was anything that thrilled us with danger without actually endangering us, such as the vast, the dark, and the obscure, for Kant, while the threat without the actuality of danger is a necessary condition for experience of the sublime, the actual content of that experience is a feeling of the ultimate superiority of human reason over the limits of our senses and imagination. Ruskin's account of the architectural sublime is that it is whatever is in buildings that expresses the power of the human mind, although for Ruskin that in turn is derivative from the power of the divine mind. Ruskin writes:

> whatever is in architecture fair or beautiful, is imitated from natural form; and what is not so derived, but depends for its dignity upon arrangement and government received from human mind, becomes the expression of the power of that mind, and receives a sublimity high in proportion to the power expressed. All building, therefore, shows man either as gathering or governing; and the secrets of his success are his

knowing what to gather, and how to rule. These are the
two great intellectual Lamps of Architecture; the one
consisting in a just and humble veneration for the
works of God upon the earth, and the other in an
understanding of the dominion over those works
which has been vested in man.[49]

Ruskin illustrates this power with examples of great
churches and cathedrals, which cannot compete in actual
size with natural features like mountains but which because
of their perceived size relative to their site can nevertheless
have an overwhelming effect, like the Superga outside Turin
or La Salute at the entrance to the Grand Canal of Venice, or
the "clear vertical fall as high as the choir of Beauvais." These
all make great impressions because "the apprehension of the
size of natural objects, as well as of architecture, depends
more on fortunate excitement than on measurements by the
eye."[50] Here Ruskin recognizes, as had Vitruvius and Kames,
that it is how we actually experience objects that matters for
their aesthetic effect, not their measurements and proportions as such. Perceived height is a particular source of
power.[51] But massiveness of masonry,[52] intense contrasts
between light and shade (here Ruskin echoes Burke),[53]
"quantity . . . of shadow,"[54] and more can all be experienced
as "expression for the trouble and wrath of life"[55] but also as
expressions of the power of the human mind and will, both
individually but especially collectively, through organiza-
tions such as church and government, to find ways to cope
with trouble and wrath.

For Ruskin, power lies in aspects of architectural
form – size, massing, light and shade – that have an

emotional impact upon us that we in turn interpret as a response to our own human power. The experience of power thus links form to content. Ruskin's conception of the lamp of beauty proper is also more than purely formal: architectural beauty lies in various ways of imitating nature, or is "derived chiefly from the external appearances of organic nature,"[56] and our pleasure in it may thus be considered pleasure in the implicit recognition of the naturalness of certain forms rather than a response simply to those forms alone, considered, again, in purely mathematical terms. Ruskin does not "mean to assert that every happy arrangement of line is directly suggested by a natural object; but that all beautiful lines are adaptations of those which are commonest in the external creation,"[57] and please us because of that association.[58] Ruskin finds beauty particularly in naturalistic or naturally inspired ornament, and although he does mention proportion he understands even that as a principle of nature, thus our pleasure in architectural proportion is a mediated pleasure in nature. As in the case of power, Ruskin's conception of beauty proper as part of the aesthetic appeal of architecture more broadly has as much to do with the content as with the form that we find in architectural elements such as floral bosses, the ribs of arches, and the tracery of Gothic windows (which also please us because of the sacrifice represented by the labor that evidently went into them).

The principle of life is also connected with labor, although not so much with the sacrifice that this expresses as with admiration for "the energy of that mind which has visibly been employed ... upon the vivid expression of the intellectual life which has been concerned" in the production of architectural works.[59] For example, there is something majestic "in the life of the architecture like that of the Lombards, rude and infantine in itself, and surrounded by fragments of a nobler art of which it is quick in admiration and ready in imitation, and yet so strong in its own instincts that it re-constructs and re-arranges every fragment that it copies or borrows into harmony with its own thoughts."[60] Here Ruskin adds an historical dimension to the aesthetic appeal of architecture: our recognition of life can depend upon seeing a building in its historical context. History is the explicit subject of Ruskin's sixth lamp, memory: here he has in mind the way in which history leaves traces on buildings, and that we can treasure buildings because of the history that we read in them, not just because of ahistorical formal features. As Ruskin puts it in one of his purplest passages, "there are but two strong conquerors of the forgetfulness of men, Poetry and Architecture; and the latter in some sort includes the former, and is mightier in its reality."[61] Architectural memory concerns content rather than form and luxurious materials, and thus adds to Ruskin's conception of the aesthetic appeal of architecture: "the greatest glory of a building is not in its stones, nor in its gold. Its glory is in its Age, and in that deep sense of voicefulness, of stern watching, of mysterious sympathy, nay, even of approval or condemnation, which we feel in walls that have long been washed by the passing waves of humanity."[62]

Ruskin concludes with the lamp of obedience, the reverence for "Obedience, Unity, Fellowship, and Order"[63] that people express through their edifices, of course in sacred architecture, but in other forms as well, for example the different varieties of civic architecture. This last principle circles back close to the first, sacrifice. But for Ruskin obedience is actually an expression of freedom: "Obedience is, indeed, founded on a kind of freedom, else it would become mere subjugation, but that freedom is only granted that obedience may be more perfect; and thus, while a measure of license is necessary to exhibit the individual energies of things, the fairness and pleasantness and perfection of them all consist in their Restraint."[64] This is a modern conception of piety: obedience is of no value if simply granted to the agent by grace, but must be an expression of the agent's own free choice.

One major accomplishment of Ruskin's *Seven Lamps* is a profound enrichment of the conception of the aesthetic appeal of architecture that makes room for emotional and historical responses to architecture while also, in the principle of truth, suggesting the connection between beauty and structural technology that would subsequently become so important. But the principle of obedience also suggests that we can take pleasure in architecture as an expression of human freedom, although not of unhindered license, which is never particularly pleasurable except perhaps for the person exercising it, and even then only momentarily. Our pleasure in the architectural expression of human freedom is also the central idea of the core chapter of Ruskin's *Stones of Venice*, on "The Nature of Gothic."

Ruskin's three volumes extensively describe and illustrate Venice's unique Byzantine-inflected Gothic architecture. The chapter on the "Nature of Gothic," located midway through the second volume, is the philosophical center of the work. Reflecting his general approach in *The Seven Lamps* of emphasizing the intellectual and emotional impact of architecture rather than more purely formal features, Ruskin argues that to call a style Gothic, "It is not enough that it has the Form, if it have not also the power and life." The nature of Gothic lies not in particular features such as "pointed arches . . . nor vaulted roofs, nor flying buttresses, nor grotesque sculptures," but in a cluster of "characteristic or moral elements." In the order of their importance, and "expressed as belonging to the building," these are "1. Savageness. 2. Changefulness. 3. Naturalism. 4. Grotesqueness. 5. Rigidity. 6. Redundance." But Ruskin is really more interested in these "characters" "as belonging to the builder" rather than the building; here they are "1. Savageness or Rudeness. 2. Love of Change. 3. Love of Nature. 4. Disturbed Imagination. 5. Obstinacy. 6. Generosity."[65] And in talking about the "builder," Ruskin means not just the architect, or master mason of a medieval edifice, but the workmen as well, above all the stonecutters of the medieval buildings.

"On the Nature of Gothic" is part of the polemic against the alienating conditions of modern industry that would increasingly occupy the later part of Ruskin's career, and which here is expressed in a contrast between what Ruskin supposes to have been the working conditions for the construction of Gothic buildings and those of classical architecture. He takes the construction of ancient buildings, whether in Mesopotamia, Egypt, or Greece, to have required "absolute precision by line and rule," with workmen trained "by a discipline so rigid, that there was no chance of [their] falling beneath the standard appointed," so that in effect "The workman was … a slave" whatever the economic arrangements of labor actually were.[66] The same would be true for workmen turning out pre-cut wooden moldings or cast iron decoration for Greek Revival buildings in a nineteenth-century factory. Their work would be instances of the division of labor leading to alienation, about which Ruskin said, with obvious reference to Adam Smith, that

> It is not, truly, the labour that is divided; but the men – Divided into mere segments of men – broken into small fragments and crumbs of life; so that all the little piece of intelligence that is left in a man is not enough to make a pin, or a nail, but exhausts itself in making the point of a pin or the head of a nail.[67]

By contrast, at least as Ruskin imagines, "in the medieval, or especially Christian, system of ornament, this slavery is done away with altogether; Christianity having recognized, in small things as well as great, the individual value of every soul."[68] In Ruskin's view, medieval stonecutters, above all in their production of capitals, which did not adhere to a rigid system of orders but could vary freely even within a single colonnade, using all sorts of vegetal, animal, and human forms, enjoyed a level of individual freedom that the slaves in the other systems did not. The "ugly goblins, and formless monsters, and stern statues" of medieval capitals and statuary are not to be mocked, "for they are signs of the life and liberty of every workman, who struck the stone; a freedom of thought, and rank in scale of being, such as no laws, no charters, no charities can secure; but which it must be the first aim of all Europe in this day to regain for her children."[69] It does not really matter whether Ruskin's image of medieval working conditions was accurate; he was offering an ideal for contemporary labor, one that would be taken up by such successors as William Morris and the British and American Arts and Crafts movements – although in the end, ironically enough, thousands of prefabricated Arts and Crafts bungalows would be shipped across the US by Sears, Roebuck & Co.

Ruskin's argument takes account of the role of labor in the production of architecture in a way that no one had before, and extends the ideal of freedom in imagination that had entered into the modern conception of beauty beginning with Kant not only to the freedom of the client as well as the architect but to the freedom of the workers as well. Another way in which Ruskin introduces freedom into his account is in his treatment of utility, to return to that, in medieval architecture, where, as he sees it, utility is to a degree freed from formalistic demands of beauty. He says that "it is one of the chief virtues of Gothic builders, that they never suffered ideas of outside symmetries and consistencies to interfere with the real use and value of what they did. If they wanted a window, they opened one; a room, they added one; a buttress, they built one; utterly regardless of any established conventionalities of external appearance."[70] Again, whether this is historically accurate does not matter; what it shows is that, as a thoroughly modern thinker in spite of his admiration for the medieval, Ruskin wanted to infuse all of the Vitruvian categories – utility and construction as well as beauty – with ideals of freedom, negatively in the form of freedom from deceit and constraint but also positively in the form of freedom of imagination and use. Ruskin's is a thoroughly modern medievalism.

4 Semper

Ruskin's idea in *The Stones of Venice* that the Gothic builders freed functionality from formal constraints of beauty ends up redeeming the Vitruvian category of utility from the neglect in favor of truth in construction and his complex view of aesthetic appeal that it had suffered in *The Seven Lamps*. Considerations of architectural function play an even more fundamental role in the theory of Gottfried Semper. Unlike Kant, Schopenhauer, and Ruskin, Semper was a practicing architect, responsible for some of the masterpieces of nineteenth-century European architecture: his opera house in Dresden, the main building of the Federal Technical University (ETU) in Zürich, where he taught for many years, and the twin Art Historical and Natural History museums on the Ring in Vienna. But Semper also wrote extensively, from early polemics in the debate over polychromy in ancient architecture and sculpture, through his mid-career essay "The Four Elements of Architecture" (1851),[71] to his massive work on *Style in the Technical or Tectonic Arts, or Practical Aesthetics* (1860–63).[72] The core of Semper's theory may be understood as demonstrating how the aesthetic appeal of architecture arises from the conjunction of the basic functions of architecture and its basic technologies for construction. As I suggested in the

Introduction, Semper does not reject the Vitruvian categories but offers a particular theory of how they are realized.

Semper's key theoretical work is entitled "The Four Elements of Architecture," but there are actually two foursomes at the heart of this work. One is a fourfold classification of what Semper calls the "moral" elements of architecture, which we can understand as functions, but ones that are fundamentally valuable to human beings, necessary conditions of human life, and are in that sense moral. These are, first, the fireplace or hearth around which human beings have to settle in their need for warmth and cooked food; and then, second and third, the roof and enclosure, that is, walls or wrap – in Semper's view, originally textiles – to keep them dry and afford privacy; and finally the mound or elevation on which buildings are raised above their immediate surroundings for defense against such threats as rising waters or the prying eyes of others. Roof, enclosure, and mound are "the protecting negations or defenders of the hearth's flame against the three hostile elements of nature" – climate, animals, and other human beings.[73] These basic functions of architecture give rise to what we experience as satisfactory forms for buildings, varying "According to how different human societies developed under the varied influences of climate, natural surroundings, social relations, and different racial dispositions" (the last because this was, after all, a work of the pre-postcolonial nineteenth century).[74] In other words, functionality influences a culture's conception of what is aesthetically appealing in building.

Semper's second distinction is among the fundamental materials available to human beings and the methods of construction they make possible. The "different technical skills of man became organized according to these elements: *ceramics* and afterwards metal works around the *hearth*," for both ceramics and metals need to be worked with heat; "*water* and *masonry works* around the *mound*," for human settlements can be protected by both moats and walls, as well as needing access to water for personal use and, in making bricks, mortar, and concrete, for construction itself; "*carpentry* around the *roof* and its accessories," because roofs were typically supported with timber framing; and finally "the art of the *wall fitter*, that is, the weaver of mats and carpets," because in Semper's view the earliest forms of walls were all woven and the patterns of weaving in various materials influenced subsequent design and decoration of walls.[75] Even as the use of masonry extended from the construction of mounds to walls, "Hanging carpets remained the true walls, the visible boundaries of space."[76] Thus the materials and methods for using them as well the primary functions of architecture led to the forms of architecture – for example, the forms emerging from the technology of weaving became decorative patterns to be used with other materials too. Semper does not talk explicitly about beauty, but what he is describing is how the forms and patterns found appealing in architecture emerge from its functional and material elements. For example, in the Parthenon "In an unsurpassed and never before attained harmony the four elements of architecture worked together as one toward a great goal."[77] He does not suggest that every combination of the four elements, or more precisely the four "moral" elements and the four material elements, gives rise to beauty, but when beauty arises it does so from these sources. Aesthetic appeal is not rejected; it is just understood as achieved through function and construction.

For all but an eccentric like Schopenhauer, therefore, the Vitruvian categories were not rejected over the course of the nineteenth century. Rather, conceptions of how these general values can be realized in practice were enriched with Kant's introduction of the idea of architectural meaning and Ruskin's even richer analysis of this idea in terms of his seven lamps, and by Semper's account of the contributions of architectural functions and technologies to its aesthetic appeal. In the next two chapters, we will see that even as both the theory and practice of architecture have developed in many new directions since the beginning of the twentieth century, the Vitruvian categories remain the most general framework for understanding architecture.

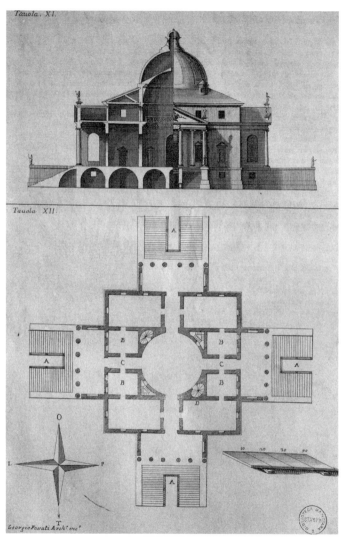

Figure 1 Villa Rotonda, cross-section and plan.
De Agostini Picture Library / Getty Images.

Figure 2a Y-House. Photograph courtesy of Paul Warchol.

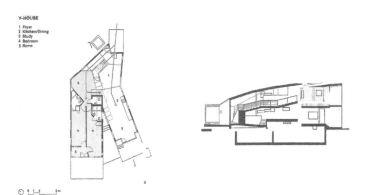

Y-HOUSE

1 Foyer
2 Kitchen/Dining
3 Study
4 Bedroom
5 Rome

Figure 2b Y-House building plan. Kenneth Frampton,
A Genealogy of Modern Architecture (Lars Müller Publishers,
2015), p. 108.

Figure 3 Sunset Park Material Recovery Facility. Shuo Yan, CC BY-SA 4.0.

Figure 4a Paul and Jean Hanna House, aerial photograph. Special Collections & University Archives at Stanford University.

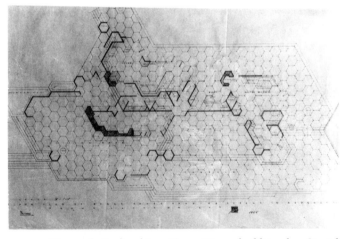

Figure 4b Paul and Jean Hanna House, building plan. Special Collections & University Archives at Stanford University.

Figure 5a Villa Müller interior. Albertina Museum.

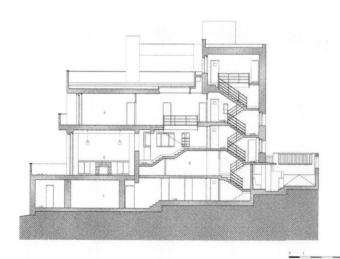

Figure 5b Villa Müller building plan.

Figure 6a Seagram building. Frank Scherschel / The LIFE Picture Collection / Getty Images.

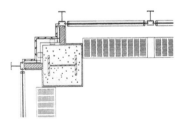

Figure 6b Seagram building plan.

3 Multiplicity of Meaning in Twentieth-Century Theories

1 Introduction

Vitruvius's *firmitas*, *utilitas*, and *venustas* were distinct but conjoint goals for any successful work of architecture. Alberti's concept of *concinnitas* unified several different values, including both formal and programmatic considerations. Kant's application of his concept of adherent beauty to the case of architecture suggested that successful works had to integrate utility and beauty even if he made no mention of good construction, while his thesis that the spirit of all fine art consists in the expression of aesthetic ideas connected intellectual meaning to perceptual form in an expanded conception of aesthetic appeal in architecture as well as other arts. Ruskin's seven "lamps" constitute a cluster of architectural values: he does not suppose that any successful building must satisfy all seven of his principles, and several, particularly beauty and power, that is, the beautiful and the sublime, might be alternatives, suitable for different kinds of buildings but not compatible in any one; but presumably any successful work of architecture will satisfy some number of these principles. These theories of architectural value are all pluralistic rather than monistic: their criteria for architectural success all require several, harmoniously integrated factors rather than some single factor.[1]

Obviously, any successful work of architecture has to satisfy multiple constraints, not just some idea of aesthetic appeal, but the client's program, the client's budget (often honored in the breach), zoning laws and building codes, and more. But what I have suggested in the last chapter is that the most interesting conceptions of the aesthetic appeal of architecture in the long nineteenth century were themselves also complex, that in its aesthetic aspect architecture appeals to us not just through visual form but also through multiple kinds of meaning. In this chapter I argue that this is true in some of the most interesting twentieth-century theories of architecture as well; they continue to work with the Vitruvian paradigm at their most fundamental level, but also continue to expand the modes of aesthetic appeal in architecture.

This has not been universally true; some architectural movements and manifestoes have been monistic, as if a single factor could determine everything necessary for a successful building. Some proponents of "functionalism" may have made it sound as if one kind of function or the other – programmatic function or structural function, to use the distinction of Eugène Viollet-le-Duc (1814–79), French architect and theorist, the restorer of Notre Dame – must be sufficient to determine how a building should look. That is obviously false; the choice of a structural technology, such as the choice of bolted or of welded steel members, the choice of energy-efficient glass, even the choice to expose as much structure as possible for aesthetic impact, can hardly determine everything about how a building looks – if the steel is not Corten steel and needs to be coated, then what color should it be painted? If the glass needs to be tinted, what color? Nor can the program or even the budget determine everything about how a building looks – if a school needs so many classrooms, so much circulation space, so many offices, all that still leaves open what colors those rooms and halls should be and what exterior sheathing should be used.[2] Even the original author of the slogan "Form follows function," the brilliant and imaginative late-nineteenth-century American architect Louis Sullivan (1856–1924), hardly thought that the intended function of a building could fully determine everything else about it, thus that successful realization of its intended function should be a sufficient condition of its beauty or architectural success. Indeed, he could hardly have thought that anything about the function of a building by itself required his elaborate decorative patterns. What Sullivan meant was just that "the function of a building must … organize its form,"[3] for example that the identical office floors of a skyscraper should be expressed by a repetitive pattern of fenestration and decoration on the shaft of those floors between the floor or two of lobby and shops at the base of the building and its cornice. Some have taken his slogan to mean just that a successful building must first of all satisfy its (that is, its client's) program, and only once that is in place can considerations about form and other aspects of aesthetic appeal be made; in other words, function, in the sense of the fulfillment of a building's program first and then perhaps also in the sense of available structural technologies, functions as a necessary but not a sufficient condition for the design of a successful building. The industrial architecture of Peter Behrens's AEG Turbine house, Walter Gropius's Fagus shoe factory, or Albert Kahn's automobile plants might seem

to be fully determined by the intended program of the building, or the design of Mies van der Rohe's various buildings
for the campus of the Illinois Institute of Technology, with
their careful, visible joints of metal and brick, might seem
as if they are fully determined by their program (chapel or
studio building) plus their technology (steel and brick, steel
and glass) – but the I-beams on the beautiful facade of
Mies's Seagram Building, which are an echo of the actual
load-bearing steel skeleton of the building hidden behind
its concrete fire-proofing, added chiefly for aesthetic
reasons, suggest that no matter what an architect's slogan
might be ("Less is more"), truly successful buildings are
functional both in serving their intended function well and
in using and perhaps displaying good materials and
rational structure, but are also designed to be aesthetically
appealing, often in many ways. In other words, the
Vitruvian triad of good construction, functionality, and
aesthetic appeal remains valid.

2 The Languages of Architecture

One common way of talking about multiple avenues for the
aesthetic appeal of architecture, especially among architectural rather than philosophical writers, has been to talk
about multiple "languages" of architecture. For example, in
the Preface to his widely used textbook, *Modern Architecture
since 1900*, William J. R. Curtis writes "I make no apologies
for concentrating on buildings of high visual and intellectual
quality," but then quickly says, "I have emphasized the
problem of architectural language, and have tried to show

how a number of extraordinarily imaginative individuals expressed the deeper meanings of their times in symbolic forms."[4] In the Introduction to the book, he writes that at the turn from the nineteenth to the twentieth century "imaginative leaps were made in an attempt at visualizing the forms of a new architecture," but then, describing what he takes to be the mood that then prevailed, that

> "Modern architecture," it was intimated, should be based directly on new means of construction and should be disciplined by the exigencies of function; its forms should be purged of the paraphernalia of historical reminiscences, its meanings attuned to specifically modern myths and experiences . . . . Modern architecture, in other words, should proffer a new set of symbolic forms more directly reflecting contemporary realities than had the rag-bag of "historical styles."[5]

What he means by symbols reflecting contemporary realities is far from clear, and often writers use the idea of architectural languages merely metaphorically, to mean the different styles of different architects or different periods – for example John Summerson's *The Classical Language of Architecture* is just a description of the compositional parts and principles of the classical style of architecture from antiquity through the Georgian period.[6] No one takes the metaphor seriously enough to consider the roles of syntax, semantics, and pragmatics, the ordinary philosophical terms for the analysis of natural language – simply put, grammatical structure, meaning or reference, and use and usefulness – in order to define their analogues in architecture.[7]

While no one has attempted to show how all three linguistic dimensions of syntax, semantics, and pragmatics could be applied to architecture, at least one sophisticated writer has used the assumption that a genuine language has all three dimensions to criticize an architectural theory and practice that attends only to one. Rafael Moneo (b. 1937), himself one of the great architects of the late twentieth and early twenty-first centuries as well as an important educator and critic, describes the early architecture of Peter Eisenman (b. 1932) – Houses I through XII, mostly unbuilt – as purely syntactical: that is, Eisenman was interested in how the most elemental formal features of architecture (lines, planes, and solids) could be manipulated, like numbers subjected to permutation and combination, without regard to much else – that is, without regard to "contaminations, whether of place, function, or building systems." Moneo writes that this "view of architectural theory as something not far removed from syntax theory becomes clear with Charles Morris's definition of syntax as 'the study of the ... relations of signs to one another in abstraction from the relations of signs to objects or to interpreters'," that is, without concern for semantics or pragmatics. He continues that this puts Eisenman "in a position that was diametrically opposed to [that of Robert] Venturi [1925–2018], who, advocating the communicative nature of architecture, suggested that it was capable of expressing the culture values that are latent in the spirit of a social group. Eisenman didn't want to hear about the symbolic."[8] That is, Eisenman was concerned with the manipulation of formal features of architecture to the exclusion of concern with location, construction, function, and

especially any form of symbolism, while Venturi was concerned above all, at least in his rhetoric, with symbolism.
This is not to say that Venturi's buildings did not often work
very well and look quite attractive to boot, unlike
Eisenman's houses, which, at least in photos, do not look
at all comfortable or even safe to move around in. It is not
uninformative to express this contrast by means of the
distinction between syntax and semantics, to the complete
exclusion of pragmatics. If we think of architectural syntax
as at least an aspect of construction, of programmatic function or use as pragmatics, and of architectural semantics or
symbolism as at least part of the aesthetic appeal of architecture, then we might loosely take these categories to be a
contemporary version of the Vitruvian triad; in that case
Moneo's criticism would be that Eisenman's syntax focuses
just on construction as one member of the triad, while
Venturi's symbolism, or at least his rhetoric about it, emphasizes only one other member of the triad, namely meaning as
an aspect of aesthetic interest, and both theories if not
practices are deficient for that reason. In other words,
Moneo is tacitly endorsing the Vitruvian paradigm.

To stay with the topic of symbolism for a moment:
William Curtis's conception of symbolism in architecture is
not defined, and Venturi's, for all the refinement of some of
his buildings, was often crude: he loved the duck-shaped
stand selling Long Island ducklings, and the face of his Guild
House retirement home (1960–63) suggested the antenna for
the TV that the residents were presumed to spend their days
watching.[9] One philosopher who applied a more interesting
conception of symbolism to the case of architecture,

however, was Susanne K. Langer (1895–1985). Langer was a student of the philosopher Alfred North Whitehead (1861–1947) at Harvard during the years when he was developing his "process philosophy," and the concept of life plays a role in her aesthetics; she was also influenced by the American pragmatist Charles Sanders Peirce (1839–1914) and the German Neo-Kantian Ernst Cassirer (1874–1945), from both of whom she learned an approach to natural language as just one instance of the more general class of symbol systems, an approach also found subsequently in the aesthetics of Nelson Goodman (1906–98).[10] Langer developed her view that natural language is but one among other kinds of symbol systems in *Philosophy in a New Key* (1942), and combined this with her view of art as expression of life in *Feeling and Form* (1953).[11] In the latter work, her key thought about symbolism in art is that the work of art presents a *virtual* object or *illusion*, which in turn constitutes "a purely and completely experienced reality, a piece of *virtual life*."[12] The idea that the primary aesthetic effect of architecture should be achieved by illusion seems odd; built works of architecture, as opposed perhaps to work that never gets beyond paper or computer screen, are as physically real as the stones or bricks of which they are made, as physically real as anything is, and do not seem like illusions – surely even the duckling-shaped farm stand did not and was not meant to delude anyone into thinking that it was an actual, quacking duck. Langer recognizes that architectural works are constructed physical objects, and that they serve "actual values" or "practical functions" such as "shelter, comfort, safekeeping," indeed so much so that "architects themselves are often confused" that such "practical considerations" are the essence of architecture.[13] No, in her view structure and function – the first two Vitruvian categories – can be no more than necessary conditions of architecture. Rather, as "a plastic art," architecture's "first achievement is always, unconsciously and inevitably, an illusion; something purely imaginary or conceptual translated into visual impressions."[14] But what Langer means by illusion or virtuality in architecture is just that the work of architecture "deals with a *created space*," that it demarcates or marks out and shapes a particular space as significant within the otherwise endless, amorphous, and meaningless extent of terrestrial and celestial physical space, the space of the scientist.[15] It is "an illusion of self-contained, self-sufficient, perceptual space ... organized as a functional realm made visible – the center of a virtual world, the 'ethnic domain,' and itself a geographical semblance."[16] What she means is that the architectural space created or demarcated out of the whole of physical space is a space that both actually houses and represents some particular form of human activity – that is what she means by calling architectural space an "ethnic domain," not that it must express one particular ethnic group in the contemporary sense as contrasted to another. Such an "architectural illusion" may be established by anything from "a mere array of upright stones defining the magical circle that severs holiness from the profane" (i.e. Stonehenge) to an elaborately "composed form" (e.g. the Temple of Poseidon at Sounion).[17] Typically, she continues, architectural works of art define the space for and express forms of social rather than individual life, thus "the great architectural ideas have rarely, if ever, arisen from domestic needs," rather they "grew as the temple, the tomb, the fortress, the hall, the theatre"; what architecture makes visible is a culture's image of some part of its "public realm."[18] Again, that is what she means by creating the virtual space of an ethnic domain. Architecture creates the space for the public life of people and expresses that life – actually, here the function and the aesthetic appeal of architecture merge, or are conjointly satisfied, in that architecture both creates the place for and expresses the character of public life.

There is a second sense in which architecture, like other kinds of art, expresses life for Langer: it expresses organic life, the living, growing, sometimes breathing and moving character of biological life. The "*illusion of life* is the primary illusion of all poetic art" but also of all visual art, including architecture.[19] Again, this might seem a strange thing to say about an art that builds ordinarily static structures out of inorganic substances such as stone, metal, and glass or only formerly living material such as wood – green roofs with growing grass have hardly been common in the history of architecture and even now such roofs are only a small part of the buildings that sport them. But what Langer means is, first, that architecture often employs decorative patterns, as do textiles, baskets, and carpets, that may or may not literally copy patterns from plant or animal life but that either way create a sense of motion and therefore life,[20] second, and perhaps more important, architecture has emotional impact, entering into the life of the humans who experience it in an emotionally meaningful way: "Everyone [who] sees great buildings, bridges, viaducts, grain elevators, chimneys, ships ... consciously or unconsciously feels their impact on his emotional life and his *Weltanschauung*," world-view or outlook on life.[21] Notice that Langer illustrates her point with examples of building types rather than styles or periods, and pays no attention to any conventional distinction between merely functional works of civil engineering or naval architecture and works of architecture as a supposed fine art (like Annabelle Selldorf in her recycling center). This suggests that function as well as form and ornament contribute to the aesthetic appeal of architecture. Emotional impact is added to the aesthetic appeal of architecture, as in Ruskin, but the Vitruvian category of functionality as well as beauty remains relevant, all of course to be achieved through construction.

Langer's approach to language had little influence on subsequent Anglo-American philosophy of language, her work has not been prominent in the philosophical aesthetics of recent decades, and I am not aware of any architectural theoretician or practitioner who made much use of her. Her work could have provided language for talking about the architecture of Frank Lloyd Wright if only he had not, as we will see in the next chapter, provided so much language of his own; and her ideas of both the virtual space and the emotional impact of architecture could be valuable additions to the theory of its aesthetic appeal. But in terms of actual influence, her work seems like something of an evolutionary dead-end in architectural aesthetics. The more prominent influence on theories of architectural aesthetics, particularly on theories of the experience of architecture, has come from European phenomenology rather than Anglo-American philosophy of language, even in

Langer's lively version of it. Langer has been worth a detour, but now I turn to that alternative tradition.

3 The Phenomenology of Architecture

Hegel's *Phenomenology of the Spirit* (1807) concerned the gradual appearance of spirit's proper self-understanding over the course of human history.[22] Edmund Husserl (1859–1938) revived the term in his 1901 *Logical Investigations* to designate his approach to the study of the structure of human representations while "bracketing" all questions about the existence of objects of those representations, thus attempting to eliminate the long-standing debate between idealism and materialism. Husserl's student Martin Heidegger (1889–1976) turned phenomenology into a radical form of realism, in which the truth of the world simply reveals itself to us if only we let it. His lectures on "The Origin of the Work of Art,"[23] originally given in 1935, during the Third Reich, and one entitled "Building Dwelling Thinking," originally given at a 1951 Darmstadt conference on the post-war German housing crisis,[24] have generated a lot of overheated prose, but at their best they focused attention on architecture as a fundamental locus for the human interaction with nature at the intersection of earth and sky, as in Christian Norberg-Schulz's *Concept of Dwelling* (1985).[25] Finally, in his 1945 *Phenomenology of Perception*, Maurice Merleau-Ponty (1908–61), although influenced by both Husserl and Heidegger, argued that human experience is essentially rather than accidentally embodied, a position that has led architects, especially the

American Steven Holl, to develop an architecture that appeals to the embodied and especially moving human being, not just to visual experience.[26]

We will return to the thought and the work of Holl later in this chapter, but the phenomenology of architecture on which I want to pause now is that of an author who did not explicitly associate himself with the phenomenological philosophers at all: the Danish architect and urban planner Steen Eiler Rasmussen (1898–1990). I call Rasmussen's approach in his enduring book *Experiencing Architecture*[27] phenomenological because, without denying the importance of functional and structural considerations in the creation and reception of works of architecture, Rasmussen lavishes attention on the multiple ways in which, as his title suggests, we *experience* architecture. Both his work in planning and building and his writing show that Rasmussen remained committed to the importance of all three Vitruvian categories. Thus, in the "Basic Observations" of his first chapter, he states that "The architect works with form and mass just as the sculptor does, and like the painter he works with color. But alone of the three, his is a functional art. It solves practical problems. It creates tools or implements for human beings and utility plays a decisive role in judging it." So successful accommodation of a project's program or intended function is not only part of its success, but a necessary condition – "decisive" – for it. This in turn means that "When an architect judges a building its appearance is only one of several factors which interests him. He studies plans, sections and elevations and maintains that, if it is to be a good building, these must harmonize with each other."[28] We can take elevations to bear primarily on aesthetic appeal, while plans and sections indicate the use of spaces in a building and circulation among them but also the actual construction and materials of the building, thus they bear on both construction and functionality. That all three factors must "harmonize" in a successful work is pure Vitruvius and Alberti.

But the point of Rasmussen's book is not to say much more about plans and sections, or construction and function; it is rather to argue that the aesthetic appeal of architecture does not concern merely its visual appearance, certainly not just a conception of visual experience restricted to formal considerations such as shape, size, proportion, and symmetry. His view is that "architecture means shapes formed around man, formed to be lived in, not merely to be seen from the outside. The architect is a sort of theatrical producer, the man who plans the setting for our lives ... . But ... his actors are quite ordinary people. He must be aware of their natural way of action."[29] In particular, in philosophical terms that Rasmussen does not use, human beings are embodied minds, their experience comes through multiple, interacting senses responding to their environment as they move, through buildings, between buildings and the outdoors, around their buildings, and so on – and architecture should appeal to all of our senses as moving, embodied beings as well as to our imaginations and understandings as they process sensory input. That the focus of architectural creation and reception can hardly be limited to form, let alone visual form, is also evident from Rasmussen's statement that "No other art employs a colder, more abstract form, but at the same time no other art is so intimately connected with man's daily life from the cradle to the grave."[30] Rasmussen's thought here is not so different from Langer's conception of architecture as creating the virtual space for the ethnic domain of human beings.

In carrying out his program, Rasmussen explores our experience of solids and cavities, or filled and empty spaces; planes as colored, visual relations such as scale and proportions but also rhythm in architecture, which appeals to our sense of motion; textural effects, which appeal to our sense of touch; daylight or light and shadow, which are to be sure sensed through sight but in a way that envelops our whole sense of being, and even our sense of hearing. He richly illustrates these topics, but his approach may be summed up by the following statement:

> Understanding architecture ... is not the same as being able to determine the style of a building by certain external features. It is not enough to *see* architecture; you must experience it. You must observe how it was designed for a special purpose and how it was attuned to the entire concept and rhythm of a specific area. You must dwell in the rooms, feel how they close about you, observe how you are led from one to the other. You must be aware of the textural effects, discover why just those colors were used, how the choice depended on the orientation of the rooms in relation to windows and the sun .... You must experience the great difference acoustics make in your conception of space: the way sound acts in an enormous cathedral ... as compared to

a small paneled room well padded with hangings, rugs, and cushions.[31]

In other words, we live our lives in and around works of architecture, and as we are embodied creatures with a multiplicity of senses and the capacity for movement, architecture can impact all of these: sight in all its richness, not just as the perception of geometrical form, hearing, feeling, kinaesthesia, sometimes even smell. For example, it is essential that a library smell of books, a restaurant of food, a church of incense, and designing for the experience of those is also part of the architect's task – Porsche has acoustic engineers whose job is to make sure that every Porsche *sounds* like a Porsche, and we can think of that as part of the architecture of their cars in Rasmussen's sense of architecture. And, as with cars, we live not just within but also around architecture – sometimes we are inside a building, sometimes we see it from the outside, enjoy its shade from the outside, or pass between inside and outside and enjoy the passage – and the architect must reckon with these facts too in the siting, design, construction, and landscaping of the building.

Given the multiplicity of ways in which buildings work on the experience of a multiplicity of individuals – inhabitants, visitors, passers-by, those who know some buildings only from engravings or photos – they will obviously affect different people in different ways. Rasmussen embraces this consequence of his approach:

There is no objectively correct idea of a thing's appearance, only an infinite number of subjective impressions of it. This is true of works of art as of everything else; it is impossible to say, for example, that such and such a conception of a painting is the true one. Whether it makes an impression on the observer, and what impression it makes, depends not only on the work of art but to a great extent on the observer's susceptibility, his mentality, his education, his entire environment. It also depends on the mood he is in at the moment.[32]

Rasmussen is not tempted by Kant's insistence that a judgment of taste, even though it is not an objective, cognitive judgment, nevertheless claims to speak with a "universal voice."[33] His approach is more like that of Kames's *Elements of Criticism*, a catalogue of numerous ways in which works of art (as we previously saw, explicitly including architecture) can please, with no argument that any particular work of art must exploit all of these elements or that any work must appeal to different people in the same way. Rasmussen explores what we might call sources or sites of our pleasure in architecture; in that regard, his approach is similar to Ruskin's. However, while Ruskin insisted upon a normative canon of acceptable architectural styles – he notoriously concluded that the choice for building in his own time would lie only between "four styles: – 1. The Pisan Romanesque; 2. The early Gothic of the Western Italian Republics, advanced as far and as fast as our art would enable us to the Gothic of Giotto; 3. The Venetian Gothic in its purest development; 4. The English earliest decorated,"[34] a judgment that has no doubt blinded many readers to the other wisdom contained in his book – Rasmussen does not attempt to come up with anything like a canon or rules for architectural success. The experiential character of his approach precludes that mistake. Rasmussen focuses on neither symbolic meaning in architecture nor on the freedom of imagination in artist and audience, as Ruskin and Kant did, but he valuably expands our conception of the aesthetic appeal of architecture while remaining within the Vitruvian framework.

Another theorist who might be thought of as enriching our conception of architectural experience, although he thinks of himself as influenced by evolutionary biology rather than phenomenological philosophy, is the architect Grant Hildebrand (b. 1934), who taught at the University of Washington. In his book *Origins of Architectural Pleasure* (1999),[35] Hildebrand argues that human beings have evolved to value the ability to hide from other humans or animals as well as the ability to see them, or what he calls refuge and prospect;[36] to value both complexity and order; and to seek security in the known as well as to take chances on the unknown, or to risk hazard and peril.[37] All of these factors are argued to have had survival value in human evolution, and thus to affect our preferences even without our conscious recognition of their evolutionary origin. They shape our experience, including our experience of architecture, rather than our conscious, conceptual thought, and that is why I associate Hildebrand's view with a phenomenological approach to architecture even though he himself does not. In a previous work, *The Wright Space*,[38] Hildebrand brilliantly analyzes the domestic architecture of Frank Lloyd Wright over the many decades of his career, arguing that Wright intuitively understood these origins of architectural   pleasure   without   recognizing   them theoretically, which is why they do not figure in his own discourse or in the teaching of his students. Hildebrand describes Wright's pattern for his houses, arrived at for his Prairie style houses by 1902 and then maintained with few departures for the rest of his career, as consisting in a cluster of features including one or more large, centrally located fireplaces; broad roofs with overhanging eaves; multiple terraces with parapets, opening from interior rooms; bands of windows, in the early years with each sash decorated with stained glass patterns; and more. Many although not always all of these features can be found in early paradigms like the Cheney (1903–4), Coonley (1908–12), and Robie (1909) houses, in his mid-career California concrete or concrete-block houses like the Hollyhock (1917–21) and Freeman (1923–24) houses, and in Wright's later masterpiece Fallingwater (1936). For example, Wright often surrounded his fireplaces with inglenook seating under a ceiling lower than the rest of the room, creating a place of refuge, while the other end of the room would open out, under a higher ceiling, with a band of windows or row of French doors, to afford prospect;[39] in his suburban houses the elevation and parapets of his terraces and even the landscaping in front of them were designed so that the owner or guest standing on the terrace would enjoy an angle of vision affording a wide view of the surroundings but a passer-by on the street could not see the person on the terrace, thus the terraces would afford both prospect and refuge;[40] the intricate stained glass windows of the Prairie houses would allow someone inside to enjoy the view outside while screening the inside from the outside, again both prospect and refuge, and these patterned windows or the varied patterns of the custom-cast blocks of the California houses would satisfy our preference for complexity while the long roofs of the Prairie houses or the simple massing of the California houses would satisfy our preference for order; the convoluted entrance to many of Wright's houses from the exterior would contrast with an easy flow among rooms once within the house, again refuge and prospect. Using the example of Wright, Hildebrand argues that our preferences in architecture, or the aspects of its aesthetic appeal, are multiple, and that we can experience architecture as satisfying in numerous ways without always understanding the sources of the appeal. Whatever one might think of his evolutionary explanation of these preferences, his phenomenology seems sound.

Hildebrand discusses Wright's "open" planning, in his early houses in the form of ready visual as well as physical access between living rooms, dining rooms, and other public rooms such as libraries or music rooms, in terms of the appeal of prospect, not in terms of freedom of movement as such or freedom of imagination more generally.[41] One recent work that does emphasize freedom is *The Aesthetics of Architecture* (1979) by Roger Scruton (1944–2020), the first full-length book on architecture by a British philosopher, indeed a very British, Cambridge-educated philosopher.[42] Perhaps Scruton would have been horrified to be discussed under the heading "Phenomenology." I discuss him under this label because his approach is also focused on the experience of buildings. Although Rasmussen's book is one of only two recent works of architectural theory cited in his bibliography, in one way Scruton's approach is narrower than Rasmussen's: he focuses primarily on the visual experience of architecture, indeed on traditional objects of visual appeal such as overall composition of elevation and the relation between details and the whole appearance of buildings.[43] However, even if Scruton's approach to the experience of architecture is narrower than Rasmussen's in its focus solely on visual experience, he goes beyond Rasmussen – but also back to Kant – in his emphasis on the freedom of the *imagination* as central to the aesthetic appeal of architecture. In particular, he emphasizes the freedom of the imagination of the *observer* rather than that of the architect, the client, the inhabitant, or other users of a building. The main argument of his central chapter, on "Experiencing Architecture," illustrates the freedom of the imagination of the observer in its account of our experience of columniation. Scruton writes: "In all architectural experience the active participation of the observer is required for its completion. Each determinacy that is offered provides the basis for a further choice, and the idea of a building that can be experienced in its entirety in only one way is an absurdity. It is impossible to banish the imaginative ordering of experience." He continues:

> Ordinary perceptual experience – the experience of animals, and our own experience of the day-to-day . . . – is compelled by its object. We are passive in respect of such experience as we are passive in respect of our beliefs. But we are not passive in respect of the experience of architecture, which arises only as the result of a certain species of attention. Our beliefs are not changed when we change the "grouping" of a sequence of columns, nor need they be changed by any of the acts of attention which we

direct at architecture. Our aim is not knowledge, but the enjoyment of the appearance of a thing already known.[44]

Scruton illustrates what he means by the reference to grouping columns with a picture of Palladio's Palazzo Chiericati in Vicenza (ca. 1550–57). The facade comprises a portico with sixteen one-story columns, the central eight standing a bit forward from the rest, supporting a *piano nobile* and mezzanine with columniated porches at each end but a filled-in wall dressed with pilasters and punctuated by windows over the central portion of the portico below. What Scruton has in mind is that one can see this facade in either of two ways: with emphasis on the horizontality of the two main floors parallel to each other or with emphasis on the verticality of the central portion, that is, the projecting porch of the portico and the pilastered wall above it. The observer enjoys the freedom to move back and forth between these two ways of looking at the facade (although the architect must also have enjoyed inventing this novel design!). Another example that Scruton offers is the Palazzo Massimi alle Colone in Rome by Baldassare Peruzzi, begun around 1535.[45] The facade of this building, which actually joins three blocks in a Y-shape perhaps not repeated until Holl's Y-House, follows the curve of the street on which it stands. Its entrance is marked by six columns, flanked on each side by the end pilaster of the walls surrounding the entrance. The spacing of the six columns is irregular, with a narrow space between the pilaster and the column at each end of the row, a wider space between that column and the next, then an again narrower space between the next two columns, then the widest space of all between the two columns flanking the entrance door. Scruton's point is that the observer has "two ways of seeing the six columns, both equally stable. We may see them as four pairs, taken together with the two pilasters contiguous with them, or as three pairs, one framing the door and the others supporting ... the outer frames of the windows on the floor above." "We find," Scruton says, "however much we divest our experience of interpretation, it retains the character of freedom which is one of the distinguishing marks of an imaginative act."[46] Scruton must mean not merely that "The act of imaginative attention is ... characterized by no specific desire to 'find out', no special preoccupation with facts," thus that the observer's response has a certain kind of negative freedom, that of not being compelled by the object to one response only, but also that the observer has a certain kind of positive freedom, that is, some control of how the object is experienced. The observer is free to experience the building in any of several ways that it allows, to vary among these ways of experience or not as she chooses. The observer enjoys this freedom.

Whether this sort of freedom of imagination is unique to aesthetic experience, it does seem an important part of it, as Kant had recognized, and therefore of our experience of architecture. Scruton says nothing about other forms of freedom that may be involved in architecture – the freedom of the architect to imagine new ways of designing buildings, the freedom of the workmen that Ruskin celebrated (or invented) in "The Nature of Gothic," but also the freedom of inhabitants to live in buildings – decorate them, rearrange them, in general use them – as they please.

There may be a reason for at least the last of these omissions. In a conversation several years ago, after a conference talk by Scruton, the British architect and author Nicholas Ray complained to me that Scruton paid no attention to floor-plans. On the surface, this comment might have meant just that Scruton talked exclusively about our visual experience of the exteriors of buildings and how we may play with our perception of them in imagination, to the detriment of the other ways in which practicing architects design and draw buildings, namely by floor-plans and sections. But there may have been a deeper truth behind Ray's remark, namely that Scruton did not pay much attention to the way in which people *use* buildings, live and work or play in them – for floor-plans, and for that matter sections, may reveal more about how buildings can be occupied and used than elevations do. Floor-plans and sections show what sorts of spaces or rooms a building has or will have, often designating the intended use for them (living room, bedroom, kitchen, bath, office, conference room), and how people may circulate within, enter and exit the building, and so on. Architects certainly pay attention to these matters of use, and sometimes, as it is said, they design buildings from inside out rather than from outside in, that is, they figure out what sorts of spaces and circulation the building should have before deciding how it should look from the outside – the great move of H. H. Richardson (1838–86) from allowing regular patterns of fenestration to determine how rooms should be disposed to allowing the disposition and use of rooms to determine the fenestration is a first step in this direction (inspired by Ruskin's remark that the Gothic builders cut a window where they needed one?). In other words, Scruton's emphasis on the freedom of the imagination in the visualization of buildings is an account of their aesthetic appeal, but comes at the cost of an adequate discussion of their function, and certainly of their construction. He adds to one term of the Vitruvian triad but neglects the others.

Finally, still under the rubric of phenomenology, let's come back to a contemporary architect as well as architectural thinker who avows a deep influence of Maurice Merleau-Ponty, namely Steven Holl. Holl has been one of the most prominent architects worldwide for several decades, known for numerous competition and built projects ranging from private homes to museums, libraries, university facilities, and multi-use complexes, as well as for his extensive writings. He has taught at Columbia University since 1981, and has documented his projects in a series of titles each of which expresses a central theme of his architecture, beginning with *Anchoring* (1989) and including *Intertwining* (1996), *Parallax* (2000), *Scale* (2012), *Color, Light and Time* (2012), and *Compression* (2019).[47] A sense of Holl's complex phenomenological approach can be gleaned from some of his own programmatic statements as well as from commentary on his thought. After his appointment at Columbia, Holl developed a new curriculum for the first-year architecture studio course. As quoted by Robert McCarter, under the leadership of Kenneth Frampton the architecture program as a whole was to emphasize "five interrelated factors ... : an interweaving of typological and anthropological approaches; a revelation of construction and expression and tectonic form; the qualifications of both type and tectonic by the topographic considerations of the site; the differentiation of public and private aspects of built form; and the engagement of parallel historical, cultural, psychological, phenomenological, and technological studies." And, in particular, the goal of Holl's first-year curriculum was "'to develop a poetic sensibility in the translation of thought into architectural composition'" by emphasizing "the intuitive, intellectual, and emotional dimensions of architecture." McCarter describes Holl's new curriculum thus:

> Holl emphasized five concepts . . . : the necessity of imposing *limits* on design in order to heighten awareness of fundamental compositional aspects; the deployment of *proportions* in composition, in particular the geometrical progression from the ratio 1:1.618 (Fibonacci series, the golden section); *composition* understood as the engagement of a series of opposing pairs – vertical/horizontal, frontality/posteriority, central/peripheral, and so on; *materials* of construction, their experiential properties, and the development of craft in their assembly; and *space and light*, and the engagement of light and shadow in the animation of form, space, material, and their experience.[48]

There are a lot of words here, and even more as McCarter expands on the further compositional concepts that Holl developed out of the painting and writing of Paul Klee: "dynamic balance, structure, and rhythm; divisional articulation; relation of musical notes and notation to bodily movement and spatial rotations," and more pairs, such as "line/plane; heavy/light; day/night; body/spirit; . . .

symmetry/asymmetry; ... path/obstruction; ... concavity/convexity" and others.[49]

But letting all the words soak in while one studies Holl's many projects both built and unbuilt, it becomes clear that Holl is working with a conception of aesthetic appeal greatly enriched by phenomenology but with equally rich understandings of both good construction and programmatic function. That is, Holl has a rich approach to form, drawing on classical forms accessible to vision – the use of the golden section permeates his work – but which is also enriched by recognition and exploitation of many other relationships accessible to vision but also to the feeling and moving body. But he is also concerned with and fruitfully employs many aspects of experience that do not obviously fall under traditional conceptions of form, such as contrasts between light and dark, light and shadow, light and heavy, and so on. When it comes to materials, he is concerned with both aesthetic appeal and with good construction, thus with both the "experiential properties" of materials but also with "the development of craft in their assembly and joining," thus with both the aesthetic and the structural potential of materials, such as polished concrete and plaster, smooth and rough metals, sand-blasted glass, and much more that he uses in ways both traditional and untraditional. And his concern with public and private spaces, with siting and topography, and more generally with "historical, cultural, and psychological" factors contributes to a broad conception of functionality, that is, how human beings experience not only the appearance but the inhabitation and use of buildings, how they move within them, between indoors and outdoors, thus between artifact and nature but also between smaller artifact (the single building) and larger artifact (the complex, the larger urban context), and so on. Further, Holl is clearly attentive to the way in which the Vitruvian categories interact in practice: his use of a material such as sand-blasted glass (one favored in many of Holl's more recent projects) is simultaneously structural (the glass itself supports weight above it), functional (the glass controls light and heat coming into the interior), and aesthetic (the glass is beautiful).

One note that is perhaps less prominent in Holl's discourse as well as design is the linguistic, although at least some of his early projects, such as the unbuilt row of houses for different tradespeople (the Tin Bender's House, the Paper Maker's House, the Word Worker's House, etc.) are symbolic or semantic in an obvious way.[50] In general, though, Holl's works do not come as close to literally speaking as do, for example, earlier works of Robert Venturi, whose Vanna Venturi House (1964) practically screams "This is a house!", whose Guild House virtually asserts "This is a home for senior citizens!", or whose Institute for Scientific Information facade in Philadelphia (1979) all but said "We process punch-cards here!" Such assertions would not sit well with Holl's complex and subtle, multidimensional design strategy. At the same time, even if Holl himself does not go in for overt symbolism, his multidimensional conception of architectural experience would certainly *allow* for intellectual meaning to interact with sensory experience in an enriched idea of architectural beauty.

Even with his frequent use of the classical proportion of the golden section, Holl's projects do not look anything like classical architecture, as we saw from our introductory comparison of Palladio's Villa Rotonda and Holl's Y-House. Nor do his projects tend to look very much like each other, as do those of architects working in a well-defined classical tradition, such as Palladio in the Renaissance, McKim, Mead, and White early in the twentieth century, or, in a very different vein, the buildings of Frank Gehry. But Holl's work shows how useful and vital the Vitruvian categories remain for both creating and experiencing, once the potentials of those categories are developed and extended as they – inevitably – have been by technological progress and change. There were no airports or stainless steel in ancient Rome but it still makes sense to think about how an airport, a recycling center, or a scientific research institute (like Venturi's ISI or Louis Kahn's Salk Center [1965]) can achieve good construction, functionality, and aesthetic appeal through changing technological, intellectual, and cultural developments and through the imagination and creativity of individual architects, their structural engineers and interior designers, and sometimes even their clients.

4   Words and Works

Modern Architecture and Traditional Values

1 From Vitruvius to Now

Frank Lloyd Wright published a series of papers in the *Architectural Record* entitled "In the Cause of Architecture." In May, 1914, he wrote:

> "Nature has made creatures only; Art has made men."
> Nevertheless, or perhaps for that very reason, every
> struggle for truth in the arts and for the freedom that
> should go with that truth has always had its own peculiar
> load of disciples, neophytes, and quacks.[1]

Part of Wright's goal in this essay was to defend his own apprentices from the unreasonable criticism that they were not as brilliant as he. But he was right to worry that talk of freedom and truth in architecture could easily become quackery, because these terms can mean so many different things that they might end up meaning nothing. That would be too bad, for I have been arguing that the Vitruvian triad of good construction, functionality, and aesthetic appeal continues to be a useful framework for thinking about architecture precisely if we interpret it in light of both truth and freedom: truth can enter into our conception of good construction, as in Ruskin, and into our conception of aesthetic appeal, beginning with Kant;

freedom of the imagination can enter into our conception of aesthetic appeal, but also into the use of technology; freedom of use, particularly of the use of spaces by their inhabitants at any time and over time, can enter into our conception of functionality. In this chapter I want to look at both the work and the rhetoric of some of the best-known architects of the twentieth century – chiefly Wright himself, Adolf Loos, and Mies van der Rohe – to illustrate and defend my argument.

2 Wright

Frank Lloyd Wright (1867–1959) lived a very long life, and practiced architecture for most of it – seventy-two years from his apprenticeships, above all with Louis Sullivan, until his dying day. He finished more than three hundred buildings, put many more projects on paper, and wrote voluminously. "Free" and "freedom" were among his favorite words. Another of his favored words, and his own preferred designation for his approach to architecture, was "organic." None of these are Vitruvian terms. And none of Wright's built work – from the Prairie School houses up until 1909, through his great works of the 1920s and 1930s, such as the Imperial Hotel in Tokyo, Fallingwater, or the S. C. Johnson Company buildings in Wisconsin, to his final visionary works, such as the Guggenheim Museum in New York and the posthumously completed Marin County Civic Center in California – looks the least bit like the Roman architecture that Vitruvius described or the neoclassical work from the Italian Renaissance to eighteenth-century and even present-day

Britain and North America inspired by Alberti and Palladio. Apart from the earliest house that can be attributed to Wright, the Charnley House, designed while he still worked in the Adler and Sullivan office (1891–92), there is not a classical column to be found in his work. While the current open floor-plan of every new house or renovation in American domestic architecture is due to the influence of Wright, the current fad for separating living and dining spaces with a pair of Tuscan columns is certainly not. Yet we can make sense of both the strengths and the weaknesses of Wright's work by seeing how even his very different literary rhetoric and visual style can be approached through the refined Vitruvian framework proposed here.

In the first of the essays "In the Cause of Architecture," published in March 1908, as his successful, primarily residential practice based in the Chicago suburb of Oak Park and focused in the Mid-West was about to go up in the flames of romantic scandal, Wright stated six principles for his "organic" architecture. This approach was *inspired* by nature but not patently *imitative* in the way in which, say, the Corinthian capital was supposed to copy an acanthus bush growing out of a basket on a young girl's grave, or imitative of natural forms in the way the contemporaneous Art Nouveau architecture in Europe or the decoration of his own "Lieber Meister" Sullivan had been. Wright's claim was that his buildings fit into nature in the way they sit on the earth and flow from indoor rooms to outdoor gardens; that they allude to nature, for example that the long, low roofs of some of the Prairie style houses allude to the flat plains of Illinois or the gentle hills of Wisconsin;

but above all that everything about his houses, from floor-plan to decoration, evolves from an organizing idea in the way an oak grows from an acorn. He stated these principles:

> 1. – Simplicity and Repose are qualities that measure the true value of any work of art.
>
> But simplicity is not in itself an end nor is it a matter of the side of a barn but rather an entity with a graceful beauty, with an integrity from which discord, and all that is meaningless, has been eliminated. A wild flower is truly simple.[2]

It is the principle and organization of a building that is like an organism, not its superficial appearance or decoration. In particular, Wright argued, simplicity was to be achieved through six more particular principles, which he in fact adhered to throughout his decades of practice: the open plan, that a building should contain as few separate rooms "as will meet the conditions which give it rise," that is, its program or intended function, and in particular in a private home the main living floor[3] should contain only three rooms, namely living room, dining room, and kitchen, "with the possible addition of a 'social office'," that is, a formal reception room, replaced in later decades with a private "study"; that "Openings should occur as integral features of the structure and form," thus not be framed in the classical way; that excessive detail should be spared; that "appliances and fixtures," for example lighting, should always be an integral part of the design; that pictures (or sculptures) should also be "incorporated in the general scheme"; and that "most or all of the furniture" should be "built in as part of the original scheme."[4] Having amplified the first main principle in this way, Wright then stated his five other main principles without such detail:

> II. – There should be as many kinds (styles) of houses as there are kinds (styles) of people and as many differentiations as there are individuals. . . .
>
> III. – A building should appear to grow easily from its site and be shaped to harmonize with its surroundings if Nature is manifest there, and if not try to make it as quiet, substantial and organic as She would have been were the opportunity Hers.
>
> IV. – Colors require the same conventionalizing process to make them fit to live with that natural forms do; so go to the woods and fields for color schemes. Use the soft, warm tones of earths and autumn leaves in preference to the pessimistic blues, purples or cold greens and grays of the ribbon counter . . . .
>
> V. – Bring out the nature of the materials, let their nature intimately into your scheme . . . . Reveal the nature of the wood, plaster, brick or stone in your designs; they are all by nature friendly and beautiful . . . .
>
> VI. – A house that has character stands a good chance of growing more valuable as it grows older while a house in the prevailing mode, whatever that mode may be, is soon out of fashion, stale, and unprofitable.[5]

This is what Wright means by organic architecture: that the siting of a house (or other building), its organization, its materials and construction, its furnishing and decoration should all be cohesive; that it should adopt from and allude to nature without simply imitating it or, we might add, attempting to refer to it; and also that it should fit in with the lifestyle and life cycle of its owners and users, that is, be suited to (Wright's idealization of) family life and also their economic life, thus should be a sound investment.

Wright's language is not Vitruvian. But there is a hint of the Vitruvian triad in this passage from Wright's second essay "In the Cause of Architecture" six years after the first, perhaps somewhat submerged in this case in his defensive rhetoric:

> And this thing that eludes the disciple, remains in hiding from the neophyte, and in the name of which the broker seduces his client – what is it? This mystery requiring the catch phrases of a new language to abate the agonies of the convert and in the name of which ubiquitous atrocities have been committed, with the deadly enthusiasm of the ego-mania that is its plague? First, a study of the nature of the materials you elect to use and the tools you must use with them, searching to find the characteristic qualities in both that are suited to your purpose. Second, with an ideal of organic nature as a guide, so to unite these qualities to serve that purpose, that the fashion of what you do has integrity or is *natively fit*, regardless of preconceived notions of style. *Style* is a by-product of the process and comes of the man or the mind in the process . . . .
>
> It is obvious that this is neither ideal nor work for fakirs or tyros; for unless this process is finally so imbued, informed, with a feeling for the beautiful that grace and proportion are inevitable, the result cannot get beyond good engineering.[6]

Wright is defending his "organic" architecture, but what he is actually saying is Vitruvian: the construction of a building must suit its materials; the construction must suit the purpose of the building; the style and beauty of the building will arise from that, but structural and functional success are only necessary, not sufficient conditions, for beauty. For that, grace and proportion that can only come from the architect's "feeling for the beautiful" are also necessary. These three goals can be realized in many different styles – over his long career, Wright achieved them in the Prairie style, sometimes with a Japanese or even a Tudor inflection; in his concrete or concrete-block style of the 1920s, sometimes with a Mayan accent; in his "Usonian" style of the 1930s and beyond; sometimes with no nameable influences at all other than the natural setting, as in Fallingwater in the Pennsylvania woods or Taliesin West in the Arizona desert. But a genuine style can emerge only from the realization of the Vitruvian goals, and must be a product of a genuine artist. It cannot be lifted from a pattern book.

In the passage from Wright's second essay "In the Cause of Architecture" with which this chapter began, Wright also invoked truth and freedom. It is easy to see what he meant by truth, and that here he is following in the footsteps of Ruskin, as different as any of his buildings early or late look from those more immediately inspired by Ruskin, such as the Oxford Museum of Natural History (Deane and Woodward, 1860) or Memorial Hall at Harvard (Henry Van Brunt, 1866–78). He meant not propositional truth, making a true assertion about anything, but expressing the nature of the materials of the building, not making them look like anything other than what they are, while integrating them into the structure and decor of the building. He also meant that the form of the building should express the building's function, although this could be interpreted quite liberally, especially as Wright's career progressed. The Guggenheim Museum does not look like anyone's idea of an art museum, even a modern art museum; rather it expressed Wright's long fascination with circles, spirals, and ziggurats. But the massive chimneys of his houses over the massive fireplaces within (see the Robie House or Fallingwater, or his Wisconsin home at Taliesin East, 1911–25); the roof like hands folded in prayer of the Unitarian Church of Madison, Wisconsin (1945–51) or the roof like Mount Sinai of Beth Sholom Synagogue in Elkins Park, Pennsylvania (1953–59) can certainly be interpreted as expressing the domestic or religious function of those buildings as well as being dramatic forms.

But what about freedom? Freedom can mean many different things, and it is often clearer what freedom is freedom *from* than what it is freedom *to*. Wright surely means several different things by the freedom he claims, but here is where tension between his thought and his practice also emerges. Two things that Wright can mean by freedom are obvious, neither of which has yet been broached in our insertion of the concept of freedom into the Vitruvian framework. One thing is the freedom of architecture from its tradition, specifically its freedom from the historical styles that prevailed for so long and came to full flower in the nineteenth-century historicism of classical, Gothic, Egyptian, Chinese, and Japanese revivals or styles. Wright's assertion in the 1914 essay that style should emerge from the work organically rather than be applied to work like a coat of paint is one way of asserting this freedom. Here the architect's freedom to create his own style can be considered the complement to his liberation from traditional styles, although that might include the freedom to use elements of a traditional style without buying into an entire system of design. Wright never stooped to the post-modern practice of the 1980s of using, for example, a classical column without its whole system of parts and proportions, or a Chippendale top on a building rather than a piece of furniture (Philip Johnson's infamous AT&T Building of 1984). He invented his own decorative schemes, but he was not afraid to draw inspiration from Tudor half-timbering (Hickox House, 1900), the upturned edges of East Asian roofs (Dana House, 1902–4), or Mayan decoration (Hollyhock House, 1917–21), or even more loosely from Egyptian massing in the magnificent Larkin office building (1904–6) or Egyptian columns in the S. C. Johnson administration building (1936–39). But he also fully transformed such elements into his own structural and decorative schemes rather than simply adopting the traditional styles from which they might have come. When he used elements of traditional style at all, he used them organically.

A second obvious form of freedom in Wright's work beginning very early is the free floor-plan. As William Jordy wrote of the Robie House, "Interior spaces open broadly into one another to create a flowing continuity within, whether experienced visually or through physical movement."[7] This is a form of freedom *from*, namely freedom from the well-defined, single-purpose rooms of Victorian design – formal parlor, family parlor, dining room, if rich enough breakfast room in addition to dining room, master's room, mistress's room, and so on. It is obviously also a form of freedom too, namely freedom to move around the house or office unencumbered by dividers – for both the Larkin building at the beginning of the century and the Johnson building in the 1930s include large open spaces rather than cubicles for much of their workforces, anticipating the open offices more recently associated with "tech." The move to open floor-plans was facilitated by technological developments: small rooms with doors were needed when only a few of them were heated by fireplaces and became obsolete with the onset of central heating and air-conditioning (the house in which I am writing this, built in 1855, has doors between the central hallway and the living room; no house built since 1900 would have them). Wright's move to more open floor-plans was not unanticipated, having been begun by H. H. Richardson in the 1870s and 1880s. Neither was it immediate; Wright's Prairie School floor-plans from the 1900s are certainly not yet as open as his plans from the 1930s through the 1950s: compare examples such as the Willits House (1902–3) or Coonley House (1908–12), where the flow is primarily between the living and dining rooms, to those like Fallingwater, the first Herbert Jacobs House (1936–37), or the great Paul and Jean Hanna House (1935–37) (Figure 4), where there tends to be much more of a single space for living, with even the kitchen barely separated from the large, multipurpose space and where, in the last, even though the bedrooms remain separate from one another, they all open to a single common outside area, when in the earlier Prairie School houses individual rooms often had their own terraces. This kind of freedom, basically freedom of movement within the house and between the house and nature, did not remain unique to Wright; we find it in Mies van der Rohe's designs of the 1920s, culminating in the great Tugendhat House (1930), where the separations between the living room, study, and dining room are more hints – a slab of onyx, a curve of mahogany – than actual floor-to-ceiling walls with doors, in the houses of Rudolph Schindler and Richard Neutra, both of whom worked in Wright's office early in their careers, and it has continued to dominate much housing and design ever since. The first thing every couple requests on an HGTV home improvement show, no matter what the vintage of the house they are about to renovate, is an open floor-plan with no formal dining room. Even the so-called "colonials" (center entrances with a couple of columns or clapboard siding) that sadly continue to dominate recent and new home construction, certainly in New England, harbor such open floor-plans, little as that has to do with the allusions to traditional style in the center entrance or clapboard siding of these houses.

But Wright also means freedom at more abstract levels. His argument about style in the 1914 paper implies that the artist – the architect – should have freedom of imagination; his list of principles in the 1908 paper implies that the audience for the artist's work – the client or user – should have freedom in the use of the building: his statement that there should be as many kinds of buildings as there are different individuals at least suggests that each building should be tailored to its client and therefore to its expected users, that is, the client and/or others whom the client expects to use the building. In a 1945 collection, *When Democracy Builds*, Wright stated that "a new Freedom would consist largely in this fresh opportunity to have and hold his own shelter ... free to come and go conveniently."[8] One can assume that this means that the building must suit the client's expected pattern of use (functionality), but the original statement suggests that the building should suit the client's taste (aesthetic appeal) as well, and it seems natural to add that it must be well-constructed so as to fulfill both of these aims for a reasonably expected period of time (good construction) – indeed, Wright's sixth principle made it explicit that buildings should retain their value over a long period of time, including possible resales, and this of course can only be accomplished through sound materials and construction. The question is how satisfying these goals comports with the freedom of the *artist's* imagination as part of or the condition of architectural beauty? (And for that matter, how is the freedom of choice of the original client to be reconciled with that of future buyers? An issue every time one makes a design or decorating choice.)

Wright was notorious for ignoring clients' budgets, often bringing projects in at double or more the original estimates, and this can be considered an affront to functionality from the client's point of view. He was also notorious for indifference to practical problems resulting from poor construction – thus the famous anecdote that when the owner of Johnson Wax, one of Wright's best clients in his later career, and for whom Wright had also built a new residence (Herbert F. Johnson House, 1937–39), called to complain that the roof was leaking on him during a dinner party, Wright told him just to move his chair a few inches. These sorts of design decisions could be considered direct affronts to good construction that in turn damaged the functionality of the building, although sometimes these sorts of problems arose from Wright's penchant for pushing existing methods of construction to or beyond their limits – had he been able to install radiant heating with the plastic tubing that is now used, floors might not have had to be torn up when the heating needed to be repaired;[9] that the dramatic cantilevered patios of Fallingwater had to be rebuilt at great cost six decades after Wright first built them, it might be argued, was due not so much to poor engineering in the first place but rather to his having attempted to do something that could not quite be done with the materials and techniques available in the 1930s. But here Wright might still be criticized for having allowed his aesthetic vision, in the case of the Fallingwater terraces, or functionality, in the case of radiant heating, to outstrip the quality of construction possible with the materials and techniques available to him. The same might have been true in the case of the unprecedented design of the Guggenheim Museum, but here Wright had a brilliant contractor and was willing to compromise enough to produce something approximating his artistic vision that has physically stood up pretty well.[10] Sometimes Wright settled for what he could do with current technology, as when he designed folded roofs because wood could not curve in the way that metal later would for Frank Gehry; sometimes a way could be found to build what he envisioned, as at the Guggenheim; but sometimes he pushed beyond what could be properly done at the time.

But the case of the Guggenheim brings us back to the basic question: there has always been argument over just how well the Guggenheim functions for the display of paintings, and in general terms this is a tension between the artistic vision of the architect and the needs as well as the taste of the client and clientele. This question also arose with regard to private homes, where Wright designed and built in furniture and lighting and exercised control over what artwork was displayed and how. Here again legend says he ignored the wishes of the client – if he was an overnight guest in a home he had designed, the homeowners might awake in the morning to find that Wright had put back in its original place anything they had dared to move. Wright was aware of this tension early on, and attempted to resolve it, but his resolution seems very much to favor the architect:

> This matter of individuality puzzles many; they suspect
> that the individuality of the owner and occupant of a
> building is sacrificed to that of the architect who imposes
> his own upon Jones, Brown and Smith alike. An architect
> worthy of his name has an individuality, it is true; his
> work will and should reflect it, and his buildings will all
> bear a family resemblance one to another. The
> individuality of an owner is first manifest in his choice of
> his architect, the individual to whom he entrusts his
> characterization. He sympathizes with his work; its
> expression suits him and this furnishes the common
> ground upon which client and architect may come
> together. Then, if the architect is what he ought to be,
> with his ready technique he conscientiously works for the
> client, idealizes his client's character and his client's tastes
> and makes him feel that the building is his as it really is to

such an extent that he can truly say that he would rather have his own house than any other he has ever seen. Is a portrait, say by Sargent, any less a revelation of the character of the subject because it bears his stamp and is easily recognized by any one as a Sargent?[11]

Wright strives to balance the freedom of the artistic imagination of the architect with the aesthetic and the practical freedom of the client, but does he really do it? The client does typically have a free choice of architects and tries to choose one whose previous projects she likes as well as who promises to realize the client's program and work with the client's budget. But Wright's talk of the architect's "idealization" of his client's character suggests that it will be the architect's interpretation of the client's needs and taste that is dispositive, not necessarily the client's own interpretation of her needs and taste. And in real life, it will often be difficult for a client to break off the relationship once she has already invested a considerable sum in the architect's plans, and she may end up throwing good money after bad.

We might say that preserving freedom that is in some sense equal for all involved is the fundamental form of all moral and political problems, and it is always hard to achieve to the satisfaction of all parties. But once the initial choice has been made, it may be especially hard to achieve in the architect–client relationship, especially if the architect is famous for his work as well as authoritative in his manner, both of which Wright was from very early on. Of course, if the architect is sufficiently famous, the client may be so happy to own a Wright that she will be willing to overlook a lot of problems in both construction and function, just as for many years owners of Jaguar cars tolerated the constant repairs of their electrical systems in order to enjoy their elegant design.

Wright pushed for freedom in many ways: for freedom from traditional styles, for freedom of movement within his buildings and between his buildings and their gardens or nature more generally, for freedom from the limits of existing technology, and above all for freedom in the pursuit of his own artistic vision. He recognized the need to reconcile the latter with the freedom of his clients, and sometimes succeeded in that and sometimes did not. Both his successes and his failures can be analyzed in terms of how well he realized the ideals of construction, functionality, and aesthetic appeal as long as those categories are understood sufficiently abstractly. Wright drastically departed from the appearance of Vitruvian architecture, but his work is no more immune to assessment from the standpoint of the Vitruvian values than is any other.

Another twentieth-century architect whose work also departed radically from the superficial appearance of Vitruvian architecture, but who in some regards might have been more attentive to the Vitruvian values than was Wright, is Adolf Loos.

3 Loos

Freedom – for architect, client, but also, in the Ruskinian tradition, workmen – within a Vitruvian framework of equal emphasis on materials and construction, functionality, and sheer beauty is the key to the thought and work of Adolf

Loos (1870–1933). Loos was born, in what is now Brno in the Czech Republic, a few years after Wright; like Mies van der Rohe, who would later build his greatest house in Brno, Loos was the son of a stonemason, and respect for his materials, not just stone such as marble and onyx but wood, brick, and in due course steel and glass, was in his blood. Loos's education was very intermittent, and his primary training in the office of a classicist architect, Carl Mayreder (1856–1935), began only when he was already twenty-six; unlike his Austro-Hungarian contemporaries Josef Hoffman (1870–1956; Loos met Hoffman in high school, but they were more rivals than friends) and Jošef Plečnik (1872–1957), Loos did not train with the dominant Viennese architect Otto Wagner (1841–1918).[12] Before getting the job with Mayreder Loos had spent three years in the US, beginning at the 1893 Columbian Exposition in Chicago. There he would have seen work of Louis Sullivan as well as the neoclassical buildings and plan led by Daniel Burnham (1846–1912), but there is no record that he met Sullivan or Sullivan's then-employee Wright. Loos never did meet Wright, and his own mature style for multilevel houses with plain white exteriors and interiors decorated with rich woods and marbles was well on its way by the time Wright's work became known in Europe through the great "Wasmuth" folios of 1901–11.[13] Loos was not as long-lived as Wright, nor as prolific: his completed projects count in the dozens, not in the hundreds. Like Wright, however, he also wrote; indeed, while Wright was enjoying his precocious success designing homes in and around Oak Park, the late-blooming Loos was living primarily from his journalism on architecture but also on many other aspects of design, fashion, and society, and hanging out with people like the essayist Karl Kraus and the composer Arnold Schönberg.[14] When he was almost thirty he began to get commissions, beginning with the Museum Café renovation in 1899, but mostly for interior design of apartments; these included his little "American" bar (1908). His first major residential commission was the extensive reconstruction and complete interior design of the Villa Karma (1903–6), and he became locally famous for a commercial building completed when he was already forty (1910), the luxurious Goldmann and Salatsch men's furnishers in the Michaelerplatz close by the Imperial Palace (Hofburg) in Vienna.[15] Above the first two shop floors dressed in hand-selected marble, Loos built four utterly plain floors of apartments with unframed windows simply punched in; surrounded as the building was by typically ornate Viennese architecture, this was so controversial that the city authorities forced him to add the flower boxes that are there to this day. Even so Loos had these fabricated out of rich bronze with no other ornamentation. For the next two decades Loos mostly built a number of homes for prosperous but adventuresome patrons, always with stripped-down exteriors and interiors decorated primarily with rich woods and marbles rather than other ornament, as well as one sugar refinery and some social housing, before several last years of ill-health and little work.[16] Loos's houses were always stuccoed and never used the patterned blocks of Wright's 1920s California houses, although among Wright's buildings those perhaps come closest to Loos's in their massing. Loos's houses are never horizontal like

144

Wright's Prairie School houses or his later Usonian houses, so they might be closest in spirit to those 1920s houses by Wright. But all of Loos's as well as Wright's houses achieve both functionality and beauty through striking materials and striking spaces creating a distinctive sense of freedom from and freedom for – freedom from traditional styles and ornament, freedom for movement.

To make sense of Loos the concept of beauty has to be understood to include freedom, while truth may be understood to be central to his work in the form of truthfulness to or honesty in the use of materials and occasionally even in a referential sense. He states that "A courthouse must look threatening to those contemplating crime. A bank must say: here your money is being held in safekeeping by honest people," but even these claims follow the remark "A living room should be comfortable; a house appear livable."[17] Loos is not primarily interested in architecture as statement, but as solid, functional, and beautiful accommodation of human activity.

Several senses of freedom are at play in Loos's most famous text, the lecture on "Ornament and Crime" that he first gave in 1909 or 1910 and repeated several times before it was published in French in 1913 and finally in German only in 1929.[18] The essay begins with what can seem like an expression of Eurocentrism, or even downright racism: "*the evolution of culture is synonymous with the removal of ornamentation from objects of everyday use.*" Loos claims that love of ornamentation is characteristic of childhood in the individual and the species, and even criminal: the facial tattoos of the "Papuan" are at the same cultural level as slaughtering his enemies and devouring them – not criminal in an amoral child or savage, but criminal or degenerate in a "modern" person.[19] No contemporary reader is likely to come to the defense of cannibalism, but even apart from our contemporary acceptance of tattooing (which Kant also condemned as a custom of the South Seas that is incompatible with the moral vocation of human beings)[20] most will feel that cultural variety has to be respected.

However, Loos's argument quickly becomes more sophisticated than this. First, he argues against ornamentation as a "waste of human labor, money, and materials,"[21] and as disrespect for good materials and good workmanship as well. Second, he allows that ornamental patterns may be produced by craftspeople out of sheer joy for their work, and here his examples range across both European and non-European cultures. As already suggested, while the exteriors of his buildings are typically stark white stucco, their interiors are richly decorated, just not with the lavish patterns beloved by his Viennese contemporaries, even by Loos's progressive contemporaries in the Wiener Werkstätte.[22] Loos offers both an aesthetic and a moral argument for freedom from elaborate ornamentation. The aesthetic argument is simply that liberation from such ornamentation allows the beauty of the materials and their natural forms to be more fully appreciated: in his homely example, a plain piece of gingerbread, rather than a "piece shaped like a heart, or a baby, or a cavalryman, covered over and over with decoration," just "tastes better," as do simply cooked vegetables served with a knob of butter rather than those with nuts and honey over which a cook has "spent hours."[23]

Of course, the vegetables and butter have to be good quality to begin with: this is Loos's justification for his own use, although only when his clients could afford them, of the carefully chosen fine woods and marbles in his interiors in contrast to his severe exteriors. (For examples of simple exteriors with lavish interiors, see the Duschnitz [1915], Strasser [1918], Moller [1927], and, greatest of them all, Müller [1928] villas [Figure 5]; for houses achieving handsome interiors with much less expensive finishes, see the Steiner [1910], Stoessel [1911], and Scheu [1912] houses.) The moral argument is, as already suggested, that decoration is a waste of labor, materials, and money, but even more that it actually cheats the worker: decoration takes longer, but workers are not paid for it – the rates paid for example to "wood carvers and turners," "embroiderers and lacemakers" are "criminally low." "Ornament means wasted labor and therefore wasted health"; not only are the workers poorly paid but the work and the working conditions destroy their health.[24] Thus ornament compromises the freedom of the workers. However, if the ornament is a genuine expression of the freedom of the worker, that's another matter. If the shoemaker truly enjoys covering Loos's shoes with "decorations formed by sawtooth patterns and holes," and without them would lose his pleasure in making the shoes, then of course he should have that pleasure; and likewise if African weavers, Persian rugmakers, Slovak lacemakers, and "the old woman making marvelous needlework from silk and glass beads" find meaning and satisfaction in their work, then they should have that pleasure too.[25] Here Loos applies Ruskin's argument for the freedom of the medieval

147

stonecarvers in "The Nature of Gothic" to his own examples. Moreover, there is no reason why the rest of us should not enjoy their work, and thus their pleasure. Loos's houses were always furnished with beautiful oriental rugs.

A second argument about freedom running throughout Loos's writing and evident in his work is his argument for the freedom of the client from domination by the architect. Unlike Wright, Loos does not privilege the artistic freedom of the architect by confining the freedom of the client to the choice of architect. Indeed, Loos sees both architect and client as part of a larger social structure within which each exercises freedom. As always, Loos dramatizes his claim:

> A building should please everyone, unlike a work of art, which does not have to please anyone. A work of art is a private matter for the artist, a building is not. A work of art is brought into the world without there being a need for it, a building meets a need. A work of art has no responsibility to anyone, a building to everyone. The aim of a work of art is to make us feel uncomfortable, a building is there for our comfort. A work of art is revolutionary, a building conservative. A work of art is concerned with the future and directs us along new paths, a building is concerned with the present.[26]

Loos did not think that he could design the plain facade of the Goldmann and Salatsch shop and apartments to express his own vision in disregard of the tastes of either the tailors or the Viennese public; he had the support of the tailors and thought the public would come to appreciate the beauty of his simple design (which they did, and the building stands today as originally designed, although the clothing shop, alas, has been replaced by a bank branch; happily, the handsome menswear shop that Loos designed for Goldmann and Salatsch's competitor Kniže is still in use, even if their Madison Avenue shop is long gone). But specifically, Loos believed that the design of a building, and especially its interior, must accommodate the taste of the client, not simply express the ideas of the architect. He makes this point in the vignette "Poor Little Rich Man," in which an architect completely redesigns a rich man's home: "He went to the rich man's house and threw out all his furniture, brought in an army of parquet-layers, French polishers, masons, decorators, cabinetmakers, plumbers, locksmiths, carpet-fitters, painters and sculptors and in no time at all Art was housed safe and sound in the rich man's house."[27] The architect even goes so far as to specify the rich man's dressing gown and slippers. At first the client is overjoyed and thrilled to be praised and envied as a patron of the arts. But when the architect visits and berates him for wearing his carefully chosen bedroom slippers in the living room and for displaying the birthday gifts that his family rather than the architect have chosen for him, he plaintively asks "surely I can buy myself something," to which the architect answers "No you may not! Never! That's all I needed, things I didn't design!"[28] It is easy to see where Loos's sympathies lie; the house and its furnishings must express the individuality of the owner or resident as much as if not more than the architect's. The architect has his own house, and it is not for him to furnish every inch of the client's home and to put things back in the place he has picked for them if the client dares move them. Indeed the

furnishings of Loos's houses are always eclectic, with oriental rugs as already mentioned, furniture from different
periods, paintings and books from the owner's own collection, even in a few instances neoclassical friezes, although
perhaps in his role as decorator Loos may have helped the
client find some of these items.

Yet another form of freedom in Loos's work is what
he called *Raumplan*, or "space plan." This is something we
might now take for granted, but which was then an innovation, namely that the size of rooms should not be regulated
by the rigidities of traditional construction, above all by the
division of a house into stories with a uniform ceiling height
throughout each one, but instead each room should have a
height appropriate to its function. Thus a living room might
be double the height of a bedroom, a dining room half a
flight of stairs up from the living room, or even in a single-
story apartment a fireplace inglenook might have a lower
ceiling than the rest of the living room, as in Loos's own
apartment (1903). Wright also liked the fireplace inglenook
and ceiling heights to be varied as one moved through the
main spaces of the house, but Loos was much more liberal
with the multistory structure of the house than Wright: the
latter built bedrooms with lower ceilings than living rooms,
but did not stack fewer floors of high-ceilinged rooms next
to more floors of lower-ceilinged rooms next to each other
as Loos did. Loos did this in a lavish house like the Müller
villa, but also used this design in more modest houses, such
as the semidetached houses of the Werkbund Settlement
(1921), three stories in front but only two in the back, with
a one and a half–height living room sitting over a lower level

sunken by half a level (exactly the plan of the 1962 Philadelphia townhouse in which I lived with my wife and daughter for a happy decade, its blank white stucco front on the street with tall windows to the garden in the rear almost certainly inspired by Loos). Unlike Wright, Loos did not seek to liberate himself from traditional methods of construction, but he liberated his buildings from the strictures of traditional floor-plans and multistory sections. And from the start, he liberated his facades from all traditional decorations, relying almost entirely on the rhythms of fenestration for visual interest.

Thus Loos's texts stressed freedom and his buildings realized it – the freedom of the client, the freedom of the workmen, and the freedom of the architecture from some of its traditional constraints but not the untrammeled freedom of the architect. He did not talk of truth as much, but his use of materials for both construction and decoration can certainly be understood in terms such as truthfulness, honesty, or sincerity. Through these means, he realized equally all of the Vitruvian desiderata: his buildings were well-built, indeed many look as good in recent as in original photographs; his plans, especially in the form of *Raumplan*, accommodated the needs of the users and adjusted the different rooms to their different functions; and his buildings are often strikingly beautiful, their beauty being achieved by formal means such as simplicity and symmetry on the exteriors and through his use of materials in the interiors. After the early Villa Karma there is not a fluted column or classical capital in sight, but Loos's buildings were surely conceived in terms of *firmitas*, *utilitas*, and *venustas*.

151

4 Mies

Ludwig Mies van der Rohe (1886–1969), as already noted, the son of a stonemason, was the most radical yet most classical of mid-twentieth-century architects. His preferred materials were ultimately steel and glass rather than marble, and there is not a classical column or capital to be found in his work – although he did have an enduring fondness for travertine and onyx slab walls. His classicism is expressed rather in the rectangular geometry of his facades and masses, in the centrality of his entrances, in the steel-dressed columns forming the ground level of his skyscrapers, more like classical colonnades anchoring his buildings to the ground than lifting them off of it like Corbusier's *pilotis*, and in the proportions of his work, which are governed by mathematical ratios as thoroughly as those of Palladio – eurythmy of the highest order. Such buildings as the Farnsworth House (1945–51) or his final Neue Nationalgalerie (1968) can be thought of as modern versions of Greek temples in steel and glass, rising above their surroundings on Semperian podia. Mies obviously strove to realize the Vitruvian values of construction, functionality, and aesthetic appeal in modern materials and without explicitly classical decoration.

Mies did not write or talk as much as Wright or Loos – although on his first visit to America, before his emigration from Nazi Germany in 1938, a planned one-day visit at Wright's Taliesin East headquarters became a four-day stay (one can guess that Wright must have done most of the talking).[29] Mies's sparse language is not overtly Vitruvian. Like Loos, although there is no record of any contact between the two, Mies spoke in terms of truth and freedom – but as we have seen these values can fit within the Vitruvian framework. Mies invoked the idea of truth upon receiving the Gold Medal of the American Institute of Architects in 1960:

> architecture should be related to only the most significant forces in the civilization. Only a relationship which touches the essence of the time can be real. This relation I like to call a truth relation. Truth in the sense of Thomas Aquinas, as in the *Adaequatio intellectus est* [*sic*] *rei*. Or as a modern philosopher expresses it in the relation of today: *Truth is the significance of facts*. Only such a relation is able to embrace the complex nature of civilization. Only so will architecture be involved in the evolution of civilization. And only so, will it express the slow unfolding of its form.[30]

It is not evident to which "modern philosopher" Mies was referring, although, himself a non-university educated Roman Catholic Rhinelander, he had become a devotee of the Catholic philosopher Romano Guardini, and was also at least briefly interested in the philosophy of Martin Heidegger, before Heidegger's Nazism became apparent.[31]

Mies's talk of architecture truly expressing its civilization could be taken in all sorts of ways, but certainly can mean that architecture should use the materials and technology afforded to it by its current state of civilization and serve the functions or way of life characteristic of current civilization – thus both construction and function should express the architect's civilization. These general values of architecture remain constant even as the particular

materials, technologies, and activities of cultures or civiliza-
tions evolve or even radically change. Heidegger's etymo-
logically tendentious interpretation of truth – in Greek,
alētheia or "non-forgetfulness" – as self-revelation could be
interpreted in the architectural context to require the truthful expression of the character of the materials actually used
that we have seen to have been a desideratum since Ruskin,
and perhaps further the structural-functionalist idea that
beauty comes simply from letting materials reveal their
nature. Sometimes Mies makes it sound as if beauty arises
simply from truthfulness to materials and structure, as in his
favored formula, borrowed from St. Augustine, that "The
beautiful is the brilliance [or "luster"; *Glanz*] of the true!"[32]
But sometimes he clearly distinguishes between the character of materials and construction on the one hand and
beauty on the other, as when, speaking of the chapel he
designed for his Illinois Institute of Technology campus
(1949–52), he said that "The chapel will not grow old ... it
is of noble character, constructed of good materials, and has
beautiful proportions."[33] For Mies beauty is a fundamental
value of architecture alongside functionality, sometimes
achieved simply by revealing materials and structural form
but sometimes by using materials in nonstructural ways.
The mastery of Mies's architecture consists precisely in the
delicate balance he could achieve between the demands of
firmitas and *venustas*.

But before we consider some illustrations of this
claim, let's also note Mies's frequent appeals to freedom.
One statement is from a 1928 lecture on "The
Presuppositions of Architectural Creation" (*baukünstichen*

Schaffens: Mies always preferred the Germanic "*Baukunst*," "art of building," to the Greek-derived "architecture"):

> We do not need less, but more technology. In technology we see the possibility of making ourselves free, of helping the masses. We do not need less science [*Wissenschaft*], but more spiritual [or "intelligent": *geistigere*] science, not less but more mature economic energies. All that first becomes possible when the human being makes himself valid in objective nature and relates it to himself.[34]

One thing this means is that new materials and constructional technology can free architecture from imitation of the past, thus that these should be allowed to find their own forms, although this is compatible with preserving the general values and practices of past architecture: rhythm, proportion, symmetry (or in a word, Alberti's *concinnitas*) may be as valid as ever. Like Wright, Mies liked to explore the potential of new materials and technology, although, perhaps because of his more practical background, he may have been more respectful of the limits of his materials. But, perhaps even more importantly, Mies's claim that new technology should free both "us" and the "masses," that is, architects but not just architects, can also be taken to suggest something about the use of architecture, namely that it should be used to allow more people to live more freely, to have accommodation and workplaces where they can live and work more rather than less freely.

This note was struck by Grete Tugendhat, the wife in the couple who commissioned and owned Mies's greatest house (1930) for a decade until they fled the Nazi takeover of

Czechoslovakia in 1938. Responding to criticism of the house as rigid, as not allowing its inhabitants to roll up the rug to dance or play ping-pong, Grete Tugendhat wrote that she found the rooms "large and austerely simple – however, not in a dwarfing but in a liberating sense. This austerity makes it impossible to spend your time just relaxing and letting yourself go, and it is precisely this being forced to do something else which people, exhausted and left empty by their working lives, find liberating today." And she argued that the design did not trap the inhabitants in a rigid scheme fixed by the architect: "no, we have found that changes are quite possible as long as the general design is not disturbed."[35] The Tugendhats' daughter Daniela later said, as paraphrased by Detlef Mertins, that "it was wonderful to live and play in the house as a child, and that they often danced and felt free to move and to use it." This must have been based on the reports of her parents or elder siblings, including the philosopher Ernst Tugendhat, since Daniela was born only in 1946 and the family never regained the house after it was used by the Gestapo, the Messerschmidt airplane company, the Russian army, and the Czech state (though now it has been restored and is open as a museum). Daniela also said that "My mother told me that [the] experience of space was an essential quality of life in the house: while providing seclusion and privacy there was a feeling of belonging to a larger totality at the same time," and Mertins interprets: "In the experience of the inhabitants, the living room was both open and closed, extending to infinity yet finite and bounded"[36] – a pretty good image of conditions for individuals living both as they wish and in harmony with others within a family circle and beyond. Some of this liberating effect was indeed achieved with modern technology, such as the plate glass living room windows that could be completely lowered or raised by mechanisms hidden below. Of course, this was a very expensive house for wealthy people. But Mies also designed housing for people of more modest means, such as his own contributions to the Stuttgart "Weissenhof" demonstration development of 1927, for which he was also the master-planner, or his later apartment projects in Chicago and the Lafayette Park development in Detroit (1957–68); in these he also strove for liberating spaces although on a smaller scale.

Another way in which Mies realized freedom in his work was through "multifunctionality": he recognized that in modern circumstances buildings could easily outlive the program for which they were originally designed, and thus he strove to create flexible spaces that could easily be repurposed as human needs changed. In a talk with Christian Norberg-Schulz published in 1958, he said that "The purpose[s] for which a building is used are constantly changing and we cannot afford to tear down the building each time. That is why we have revised Sullivan's formula 'form follows function' and construct a practical and economical space into which we fit the functions";[37] and one of his associates in the last period of his practice wrote:

> Mies . . . believed that functional requirements may, in
> time, change, while form, once rigidly established, cannot
> easily be modified. He therefore chose a structural system
> in relation to the magnitude of the functional
> requirement as a whole rather than to their individual

and specific needs. And because he was convinced that the principle of flexibility was a modern principle, he fixed only essentials in his buildings, thereby permitting great flexibility and freedom for both initial layouts and future modification.[38]

In other words, under modern conditions the Vitruvian requirement of functionality is realized through flexibility for multiple functions over time. This is not a rejection of the value of utility, but a refinement of it. Mies achieved this goal in late buildings by hanging the load of a structure from great overhead trusses, leaving wide spaces free of interior columns or supporting walls, as in Crown Hall (1950–56) for the School of Architecture at Illinois Tech, or by using trusses within the roof structure to allow it to be cantilevered from a few perimeter columns, again leaving wide spaces in the interior in which nonsupporting walls could easily be moved around, as in his Bacardi Administration Building in Havana (1957–58) or the Neue Nationalgalerie. So freedom for Mies meant using new technology to liberate structure from the constraints of the past while retaining the values of both utility and beauty at the most general level, and in turn using structure to liberate people's activity within a building.

Now let's return to the relation between beauty on the one hand and materials and structure on the other. In the essay on "Building Beautifully and Practically!" Mies stated that:

> It appears completely clear to me that with the altered needs and new means that technology puts at our disposal we will arrive at a *new kind of beauty*. By no means do I believe we will ever acquaint ourselves with

> the "beautiful in itself." But what does a medieval saying
> so rightly express? "The beautiful is the brilliance of the
> true!" In the end even beauty is bound to reality, it does
> not float in the air but hangs on things and is
> indissolubly connected with the formation [*Gestaltung*]
> of the things of reality.[39]

This could easily be taken to suggest that beauty is supposed to arise directly from materials and structure ("the
poetics of construction"), and that no independent aesthetic considerations should enter into the design of a
building. Many have understood the structural functionalism of modern architecture in this way. But this is far
from what Mies thought, or certainly what he practiced.
A few examples will demonstrate how Mies actually bal-
anced structural and aesthetic considerations.

It might be thought that a modern building achieves
its beauty simply by revealing rather than masking its materials and structure. But in a reinforced concrete structure, an
essential material and part of the structure, namely the rebar
or reinforcing rods, is buried within the concrete and can
never be exposed to the elements; in a steel-frame building
of any size, the structural steel posts and beams must be fire-
proofed and cannot be left exposed. In early steel-frame
construction, such as the office buildings of Louis Sullivan,
the fire-proofing could be in the form of terra-cotta clad-
ding, and that could be cast in beautiful designs as Sullivan
did. By the time Mies built his 860–880 Lake Shore Drive
apartments in Chicago (1948–51) or Seagram Building in
New York (1954–58), the structural steel was covered in
sprayed concrete, which is downright ugly. Further, in order

for the frame to expand or contract with temperature changes at the same rate as other elements of the building, its columns and girders have to be set back behind the curtain wall, and cannot be at the surface of the building. So beautiful as it might seem to simply reveal the steel frame of the building, preserving the elegance of the unsheathed frame against the sky that we see during construction, this cannot be done. So what did Mies do? He attached vertical I-beams to the exterior surfaces of his buildings that served no direct structural purpose but could allude to the actual structure of the building, and thus contribute a kind of meaning to the beauty of the building (Figure 6). Mies further used these I-beams as mullions between windows in order to create a play of light and shadow that changes throughout the day – a beautiful purely aesthetic effect. And while at Lake Shore Drive he did all this with black-painted I-beams, at the Seagram Building he did it with more finely detailed bronze I-beams, which are both too soft and too expensive to be used in a structural role but which are beautiful. Mies also adjusted features such as fenestration and lighting for purely aesthetic effects. While on most modern high-rises all the glass windows or panels would be exactly the same size, in the four windows of each bay between the larger I-beams expressing the hidden actual structural columns of the Lake Shore Drive buildings Mies made the outer two windows just slightly narrower than the two central ones, creating a subtle rhythm to which the viewer pleasurably responds without even being consciously aware of the difference, like the subtle variations in the width of a classical column as it rises. At the Seagram Building, he insisted on uniform ceiling lights at the perimeter of every office that were not needed to properly light the building during working hours but which were left on so that the building would be beautiful at night. Of course, the latter sort of feature would add cost to the building in a way that the former might not, so it might take an indulgent client to allow it (which in the case of the Seagram Building Mies had in the person of the Seagram owner Samuel Bronfman and his architect daughter Phyllis Lambert).

Had we room to look at more work by Holl and Selldorf as well as other contemporary architects such as Diller Scofidio + Renfro, Tod Williams and Billie Tsien, or Grafton Architects Yvonne Farrell and Shelley McNamara (e.g. their Toulouse School of Economics, 2019),[40] we would find work that looks even less like ancient or Renaissance architecture than the work of Wright, Loos, or Mies. But we would still find that while the materials and techniques, the look, and the rhetoric of modern architecture as it has developed since the beginning of the twentieth century have moved far away from the architecture that Vitruvius, Alberti, or Palladio described and designed, good construction, functionality, and aesthetic appeal remain the ideals for designing and the norms for evaluating works of architecture. These concepts are abstract, and thus have always been and must be broadly interpreted to remain useful. The specific materials and technologies, the functions, and the aesthetics of buildings have all changed drastically over the centuries. But it remains the goal of every architect, in projects from residential renovations to grand museums, concert halls and airports, to build structures that will serve the needs of present and future users, including their need for freedom, in ways that are aesthetically satisfying, however broad and varied their conceptions of aesthetic satisfaction may be. Particular conceptions of architectural success have varied and will continue to vary radically, but the fundamental criteria of such success have not and will not.

5 Looking Forward

Hegel wrote that the "the owl of Minerva begins its flight only with the onset of dusk." By this he meant that "philosophy ... is *its own time comprehended in thoughts*," and "It is just as foolish to imagine that any philosophy can transcend its contemporary world as that an individual can overleap his own time or leap over Rhodes."[1] In other words, philosophers can uncover the concepts and principles underlying past and present human knowledge and action, but it is not part of the discipline to predict the future. Yet the boundaries between past, present, and future are themselves evanescent, because the present is all there is yet is always vanishing: what is present at one moment is past at the next and what is future now will shortly be present and then past in its turn. Thus there is no reason why the passage of time by itself should invalidate general principles. If principles are truly general they will hold in some form in the future as they have in the past and present. So if the Vitruvian values of good construction, functionality, and aesthetic appeal have remained valid from the beginnings of architecture into its recent past and the present, then they ought to hold good, at some level and in some form, into the future, although the concrete circumstances of human life and habitation will change in all sorts of ways, some of which we can now imagine and some of which we cannot. As these concrete circumstances of human life change, so will all sorts of human arts and technologies, and therefore also architecture, which combines art and technology. But we can be sure that good construction, functionality, and aesthetic appeal, broadly and flexibly understood, will remain valid categories for creating, experiencing, and evaluating architecture.

So let's think about these three categories. If there is one thing that the history of aesthetic theory as well as the clothes we wear on our backs can teach us it is that we would be fools to try to predict what we – we living now as well as our descendants – will find aesthetically pleasing and interesting at any time in the future. Since the debate on whether there are universal norms of taste began in the eighteenth century, it has been a tug-of-war between the thesis that there are forms whose beauty transcends particular places and times and the antithesis that aesthetic preferences are so influenced by local customs and individual idiosyncrasies that no such norms are possible. Recently there have been evolutionary aestheticians like Dennis Dutton and Stephen Davies and architectural theorists like Grant Hildebrand who argue that certain aesthetic preferences have been hardwired into human beings by millennia of prehistory beginning at the borders of the African savanna,[2] but also philosophers like Alexander Nehamas who argue that aesthetic preferences are so much a matter of individual development and education, with all its idiosyncrasy and serendipity, that it would be best to use the term "taste" to denote only the preferences of individuals, what we might call the aesthetic dimension of individual character, rather than illusory general norms.[3]

Some of the earliest theories of taste made conceptual space for this tug-of-war without realizing it. Thus Joseph Addison's 1712 essays in *The Spectator* on "The Pleasures of the Imagination," which might be regarded as the first treatise on aesthetics in English, identified the three basic sources of such pleasure as "*Greatness, Novelty,* or *Beauty,*"[4] and forty years later Alexander Gerard in his prize-winning *Essay on Taste* even put the "sense or taste of Novelty" ahead of the "sense or taste of Sublimity" and the "sense or taste of Beauty";[5] yet as soon as these are distinguished from each other we must also recognize that while individual objects might please primarily in virtue of one of these categories or combine more than one, our tastes for novelty, beauty, and simplicity can also clash. We might find materials and forms that we have grown used to beautiful or sublime, but the human love of novelty – whether in the artist or the audience or both – may also test and disrupt our customary preferences, leading either to their change or to the rejection of the new work. And which will be the outcome we can hardly predict. Even John Ruskin, who supposedly believed that the principles of architecture were fixed by its history, actually recognized that his own preference for what had been done in stone and wood in Gothic architecture over what was beginning to be done in his own time with metal and glass was just a matter of what he was accustomed to, and that as we got used to new materials and their aesthetic potentials our preferences would inevitably change: "Abstractedly there appears no reason why iron should not be used as well as wood; and the time is probably near when a new system of architectural laws will be developed, adapted entirely to metallic construction."[6] Perhaps we can say something so general as to be virtually irrefutable, such as that human beings will always take pleasure in some balance between uniformity and variety – but whether that means that the amorphic forms of Frank Gehry will still be found beautiful or will seem aesthetically pointless and economically extravagant fifty or a hundred years from now, as dated as the post-modernism of Michael Graves or the late Philip Johnson, no one can say now.

So to discuss the future of architecture, let's focus on the future of construction and functionality instead of beauty. But keep in mind that although construction, functionality, and beauty are conceptually distinguishable, in practice they are often achieved by common or intertwined means, as the twentieth-century doctrine that beauty should be achieved through constructional technology or the "poetics of construction" reveals. The following discussion will thus be organized around issues facing architecture now and in the foreseeable future, not directly around the three Vitruvian categories – but we will see in the end how they remain relevant.

One important trend in contemporary architecture that will no doubt continue into the future is the adaptive reuse of historically interesting and/or aesthetically appealing structures that have been rendered inadequate or obsolete by social and economic developments. Adaptive reuse can respond to declining attendance at parish churches, which may be reconfigured into apartments; to the emptying of textile mills by the movement of the industry first from the northeast of the United States to the south and from there to South Asia; to changes in logistics like the relocation of mail-sorting from grand early twentieth-century post offices adjoining central train stations, as in Manhattan and Philadelphia, to more remote warehouses near airports; and in Turin, Fiat's outmoded multistory factory was redeveloped into a mall and theater.

Some of this already happened decades ago, some still happens, and no doubt more will continue to happen; remember that the boundaries between past, present, and future are always moving, so what is contemporary at any moment will be historical at another and itself ripe for adaptive reuse at some point. Adaptive reuse is not just redeveloping nineteenth-century textile mills into apartments, but as an *Architectural Record* photo essay on "Reimagining the Past" shows, something as recent as Eero Saarinen's Bell Labs (1962–64), expanded in the 1980s by Saarinen's successors Kevin Roche and John Dinkeloo, has already been radically transformed by Alexander Gorlin Architects for a new mix of uses by software developers, law firms, investment companies, and even a branch of the county library, and in conformity with new building codes such as current smoke-evacuation requirements.[7]

Mies van der Rohe, as we saw in the previous chapter, already recognized that the function of a modern building would change multiple times over its lifetime and insisted on flexible spaces for that reason. But many recent projects involve repurposing older structures that were never intended to be flexible but turn out to be so nevertheless, or adding new construction to older construction in ways never originally envisioned. And when they do either of these things, it may turn out that there are not just functional goals being served, not just economies in reusing existing structures rather than building from the ground up (although sometimes it is less expensive to tear down and build anew than to renovate), not just environmental good that may be done by saving old materials from landfill and using less new material, but also there are aesthetic goals being served: an old building may be pleasing to us for many reasons, its age and history along with its design and detail – Ruskin's "lamp of memory" as well as that of beauty – and combining it with something new in a way that is aesthetically pleasing may make for more aesthetic appeal than either the old by itself or the new by itself would have.

One successful example of adaptive reuse has been the conversion of the High Line in Manhattan, a disused elevated railroad freight spur, into a mile and a half long linear park by the architects Diller Scofidio + Renfro, the landscape architect James Corner, and the Dutch garden designer Piet Oudolf. This project not only transformed the rusting relic of an earlier era of logistics into a beautiful park in a part of the city far from the great nineteenth-century projects of Frederick Law Olmstead, Central and Prospect parks; it has also become a tremendous tourist attraction, estimated to welcome eight million visitors per year – equivalent to the entire population of all five boroughs of New York City – by 2019, and has spurred development throughout the area, including the relocated Whitney Museum (2015) by Renzo Piano (b. 1937). By assigning a new function to a construction from an earlier age, this project not only found a new source of aesthetic appeal but improved the functionality and aesthetics of an entire part of a city.

Another widely noted recent adaptive reuse project is the Elbe Philharmonic Hall in Hamburg, Germany, by the Swiss architects Jacques Herzog and Pierre de Meuron (both b. 1950), about whom the late *New York Times* architecture critic Ada Louise Huxtable wrote that "They refine the traditions of modernism to elemental simplicity, while transforming materials and surfaces through the exploration of new treatments and techniques."[8] Herzog and de Meuron's constant exploration of new materials and techniques means that no two of their buildings look alike, and their Hamburg complex looks like neither any of their other buildings nor much like anything else. Completed in 2017 after two decades in development (and at almost four times the originally estimated cost), the building is a soaring addition of eighteen floors sheathed in glass sitting atop an eight-story brick warehouse from the 1960s in Hamburg's Speicherstadt, its harbor with many striking older warehouses that somehow survived World War II. It houses three different concert halls, ranging from 2,100 to 170 seats, a hotel, and forty-five luxury apartments. Everything about the building seems striking: its acoustics are by all accounts wonderful, its location is commanding and its appearance is dramatic, and while looking nothing like the surrounding warehouses its glass reflects and thereby celebrates them all. It may not fit anyone's preconceived idea of a beautiful concert hall, but seems to establish a standard of its own. It appears to serve its multiple functions successfully, and while it was hardly economical to build, it seems as if its ongoing operation would be economically sound (at least until the 2020 collapse of both hotel room occupancy and concert attendance due to the pandemic). And while it contains parking for 433 cars, presumably most of the guests at a sold-out concert would arrive by public transportation, thus the building makes some concession to environmental concerns beyond saving the preexisting warehouse from disposal. The Elbe Philharmonic is radically new in appearance and many other aspects, but nevertheless exemplifies the values of good construction, functionality, and aesthetic appeal.

There are many other examples of successful adaptive reuse in contemporary architecture that we could discuss, some equally successful, some more controversial, or clearly less successful. As long as the functions of buildings keep changing along with continuing changes in economy and culture like those that have allowed churches and mills to be repurposed, adaptive reuse will remain a significant part of architectural practice. And everything is connected to everything: for example, if environmental concerns about modes of transportation should lead to increased concentration of population in downtowns then adaptive reuse will become even more important than it is now, but if the present pandemic produces a long-term tendency to de-densification that in turn leads to further suburbanization, then new construction in yet undeveloped areas may become far more important than adaptive reuse – although then new uses may have to be found for underutilized office towers.

Changes in the economy, in culture, and even public health that we can hardly predict now will always be challenges for architects.[9] Two challenges that we can certainly identify now are climate change and social justice. Neither of these crises can be addressed by architecture alone, of course, but they can be addressed in part by architects and their clients from individuals to municipalities to states and national governments. They are currently being addressed in many ways and we can only hope that they will receive even more attention.

With regard to climate change, the most obvious concern is with the consumption of energy derived from nonrenewable and polluting fossil fuels in the operation of buildings. But the climatic implications of construction materials and techniques have also been and will increasingly be of concern. Both of these issues have been addressed for several decades now with the LEED (Leadership in Energy and Environmental Design) certification program developed by the nonprofit US Green Building Council since 1993, and currently applied to 83,452 projects worldwide comprising 13.8 billion square feet, managed by close to 120,000 professionals and volunteers. The LEED program provides a "comprehensive system of interrelated standards covering aspects from the design and construction to the maintenance and operation of buildings," with buildings receiving rankings from "certification" to "platinum." The criteria for ranking address many matters from site-to-area ratios, energy use, and rainwater recapture and distribution to thermal, visual, and acoustic comfort and interior air quality.[10] The LEED program has not been uncontroversial, and some studies have suggested that buildings receiving the lower levels of ranking actually consume more energy in operation than conventional buildings even if they save some in construction, although buildings with the higher rankings (gold and platinum) do better, and in any case energy consumption is not the only criterion for LEED ranking.

There are also materials and techniques being used to address environmental concerns outside of the LEED program. Energy-efficient or net-zero construction, for example with rammed earth or adobe-coated hay bales, geothermal heating and cooling, and more, can address both energy consumption in operation but also energy consumption in the production and transportation of building materials: rammed-earth construction might need energy-inefficient heavy equipment for ramming the material but may also use on-site materials and thus cut down on the release of CO_2 in transportation. Environmental pressures also affect building design and construction in ways that do not directly concern energy consumption and pollution, for example the use of nonflammable siding and roofing materials is a response to increasing danger of forest fires due to increasing temperatures and changing rainfall patterns or hardening structures against rising sea levels. Some of these considerations are more appropriate in some locales than others: construction techniques like rammed earth and the use of nonflammable materials for safety from increasing forest fires are more relevant in the western US than in the northern and eastern parts of the country, where rising sea levels and more frequent storms are instead major concerns.

Multiple factors bear on every development: for example the increasing use of cross-laminated and cross-nailed mass lumber instead of structural steel in timber-rich areas such as the US, Canada, and Scandinavia depends on technological advances, as in fire-proofing, but also has environmental implications – the wood that is used stores carbon instead of releasing it into the atmosphere as in the production of steel and concrete, and properly managed forests can replace cut trees with new ones that will continue to remove and store CO_2 from the atmosphere. The production and transportation of concrete are responsible for a significant percentage of total CO_2 release worldwide, and intensive research is currently being undertaken to develop more environmentally friendly formulations for this indispensable material for building and infrastructure throughout the world so that it will release less CO_2 in production and retain more of it once in place.

As Ruskin realized, our aesthetic responses are at least partly formed by our past experience, and using new materials and techniques for construction can present aesthetic challenges for design that will call for architectural imagination as well as engineering prowess. Sometimes new materials will present minimal aesthetic challenges: a California house sheathed in cement-based clapboard siding does not look very different from one sheathed in wood, and environmentally friendlier concrete may not look or handle differently from traditional formulas at all. Sometimes new materials will present aesthetic challenges: the aesthetics of a tall building constructed from mass lumber cannot be the same as one framed in steel, where the steel frame or allusions to it (as in Mies's masterpieces) cannot be part of the look of the building. But whatever changes are in store, we can be sure that the general considerations of good construction – construction that is good both economically and environmentally – functionality, and aesthetic appeal, however similar or different that might be to what we have previously found or now find pleasing, will continue to be the relevant factors for the experience and assessment of architecture.

Like everyone else in society, architects also have to address social issues such as inequality and injustice, although these great social ills can hardly be redressed by architecture alone. This is an issue of freedom in the most obvious sense: the right of everyone in a society to enjoy equal freedom of choice and action, and conditions such as education and healthcare that make the exercise of such freedom possible. Obviously, the products of architecture – the built environment of homes, schools, hospitals, stores, and everything else – can either exacerbate or ameliorate social ills such as income inequality, segregation, and homelessness. But, as with every other profession and occupation, there is also the issue of unequal access to and reward from the practice of architecture itself. Perhaps the day is long gone when Julian Abele (1881–1950), the first Black graduate of the architecture school of the University of Pennsylvania who became the lead designer by age twenty-five for Horace Trumbauer (1868–1938), the most prominent Philadelphia architect between Frank Furness (1839–1912) and Louis Kahn (1901–74), received little or no credit for his vital contributions to such great projects as the Harry Elkins Widener Memorial Library at Harvard University (1914), the Philadelphia Museum of Art (1929), and much of the Duke University campus. Abele received credit for the Duke chapel only when it was completed in 1950, long after Trumbauer's death; in a sign of the times, Abele himself also apparently made little attempt to claim credit for his work. The first Black architect to become a member of the American Institute of Architects, in 1923, and a member of its College of Fellows, in 1957, was Paul Revere Williams (1894–1980); he completed 3,000 projects, including homes for celebrities such as Cary Grant, Frank Sinatra, and Lucille Ball and Desi Arnaz, as well as commercial projects such as the Beverly Hills headquarters of the Music Corporation of America and the interior of the Wilshire Boulevard Saks Fifth Avenue, and public projects such as Langston Terrace in Washington, D.C. But he had to learn how to draw upside down so his white clients could look at his work from across the table rather than sitting next to him, and he would be forgotten if *Architectural Record* had not just focused much of an issue on the place of minority architects in the profession.[11] The world-renowned Ghanaian-British architect David Adjaye (b. 1966) made his reputation in the US with such projects as the National Museum of African American History and Culture on the Mall in Washington, D.C. (2016) and the Sugar Hill housing project (2015) and Studio Museum (under way) in Harlem, although these works have now opened the door to a wider range of commissions including other museums as well as residential and commercial buildings.

The place of women in architecture is also a present and future challenge for the profession, as it is for many others. For much of the twentieth century, the only prominent American woman architect would have been Julia Morgan (1852–1957), the first woman to receive an architectural license in California. But Morgan was not widely acknowledged in her time even though she completed over 700 projects. Some of her best projects, such as the Berkeley Women's Club and much of the campus of Mills College in Oakland, limited her renown because they were built for women as well as by a woman. Other women around the architectural world were better known for the "lesser" arts of interior and furniture design, such as Florence Knoll (1917–2019), and often worked in the shadows of their husbands, such as Ray Eames (1912–88, wife of Charles), Aino Aalto (1894–1949, wife of Alvar), and Lilly Reich (1885–1947, partner of Mies). As recently as 1991, the Pritzker Prize, the leading international prize for lifetime achievement, went to Robert Venturi only, in spite of the fact that he had always shared his practice with his wife, Denise Scott Brown (b. 1931), and in spite of his own protests. The Pritzker Prize went to a woman, Zaha Hadid (1950–2016), only after the turn of the twenty-first century, in 2004. To be sure, at present some of the nationally and internationally most prominent architects are women: some of their names have already been mentioned, such as Billie Tsien, Elizabeth Diller, Annabelle Selldorf, and the 2020 Pritzker Prize winners Yvonne Farrell and Shelley McNamara; but there are others, such as Jeanne Gang, and how should we classify the multitalented architect, landscape architect, sculptor, and artist Maya Lin, who won the competition for the Vietnam War Memorial with her breathtaking design as a 21-year-old Yale undergraduate? But as in many other professions, women still face a harder way forward than men, and women in leadership positions in the large corporate firms remain rare.

The challenges for architects to contribute to social justice by their products are at least as great as the challenge to practice in a socially just way. Many of the ills of the built environment go well beyond the power of architects to heal: segregated housing patterns produced by government-sanctioned mortgage-lending practices as well as by individual prejudice,[12] run-down private and public housing in areas with large minority populations, poor transportation between such areas and areas with good employment possibilities, and substandard schools have been produced by a range of social forces and economic and political decisions, not by the architectural profession. Nevertheless, architectural choices have sometimes contributed to social ills, and when they do have the opportunity to design public housing, for example, architects have the chance to do better than they have sometimes done in the past. For example in the US and Britain Le Corbusier's vision of the city of the future consisting of towers spaced in splendid isolation on otherwise featureless greenswards, enthusiastically accepted by many architects at the time, found its fullest realization in public housing projects in the US and Britain in the 1950s and 1960s, but quickly succumbed to problems such as isolation from or destruction of existing neighborhoods with jobs, shopping, and employment, poor transportation links to the rest of their cities, and difficult and inadequate maintenance. Some of these projects, originally built with great fanfare, had to be torn down within a couple of decades, such as the notorious Pruitt-Igoe project in St. Louis and Cabrini-Green in Chicago.

Where the political will to build such housing exists at all, architects are beginning now to do better and must do so in the future. A recent issue of *Architectural Record* devoted to "The Housing Crisis: Multifamily Models from around the World" provides examples of more promising projects in a wide range of places. One article describes how New York, "The nation's largest city[,] looks to accommodate growth without displacing low- and middle-income residents," although it concerns political issues and difficulties, such as tension between city-level rent-control regulations and state-level rent-stabilization programs and percentages of below market-rate apartments required in market-rate projects, as much as innovative architectural designs. "Living in the U.S.: At What Cost?" discusses the problem of ever-rising building costs pitted against stagnant wages for low- and mid-income people; this can be addressed politically with programs such as rent subsidies, but also poses a challenge for architects to find cost-efficient ways to build good housing.

Another article describes attempts to address homelessness. This is not a problem caused exclusively or even primarily by the cost of building and maintaining homes; in good part, it was caused by changes in the social approach to the treatment of mental illness in the 1980s, and has subsequently been exacerbated by precarious employment. But architects can help; one illustration shows a typical encampment of tents and cardboard boxes under a highway overpass in Oakland, California, replaced by a well-laid-out community of enhanced garden sheds with utilities such as the electricity and running water that most people in developed countries can take completely for granted. The garden sheds might have come from Home Depot, but architects were involved in transforming them into a pleasant little community where people could live with some self-respect. Of course, it will take more than architects to maintain them. Neither the problems nor the solutions are unique to the US; another article rounds up "International Models of Urban Housing," and illustrates innovative projects such as attractive multistory housing in Johannesburg, South Africa, utilizing the internationally ubiquitous material of shipping containers, and a development in London based on the traditional pattern of tightly packed terraced houses but with much more attention to natural light, low-maintenance materials that will prevent rapid deterioration of the homes, outdoor space, renewable energy, and sheer visual interest than has been typical for moderate-cost housing.[13] Projects like the latter depend upon good policies but equally upon architectural imagination and innovation. One thing that we can safely predict is that the latter will only become more necessary as the world faces up not only to continuing patterns of social and economic injustice but to the ever-increasing reality of climate change and all of its consequences. And growing social justice in housing is just one challenge for society as a whole and the architectural profession as part of it; other challenges include bringing parks to underserved, poorer, often minority neighborhoods, rethinking juvenile detention centers and penal facilities more generally, and more.[14]

An article entitled "Fast Forward: Architecture in 2031" is a "speculative fiction" about a practice led by a Black woman architect ten years into the future. But it describes means that are already available and ends that are already pressing: "Their team was facile with sophisticated digital modeling, enhanced by generative design through algorithms, simulations, and principles of digital fabrication," and with such means "They created buildings that actually improved social conditions, used energy responsibly, met strict construction budgets and schedules, and supported the local economy."[15] This description of the means and ends of the fictional firm does not use Vitruvian language, but two of the traditional values of architecture are clearly being imagined as realized in this scenario. Innovative methods of design and fabrication are still methods for good construction, and responsible energy use and supporting the local economy contribute as much to functionality as do meeting the needs of individual occupants. Building within budget and on time, which can also fall under the general rubric of functionality, was just as much a concern in the time of Vitruvius as it is today and will be a decade from now or in any foreseeable future. What the fiction does not mention is the aesthetic appeal of the imaginary architecture of 2031. But there is no reason to think that people ten years from now, or fifty or a hundred years from now, or any number of years from now when human beings still exist, will be any less concerned to live and work in aesthetically pleasing environments than we are now – whatever in particular they may happen to find aesthetically pleasing. In other words, what counts as good construction, functionality, and aesthetic appeal will change, as it has changed in the past, with changing circumstances – economic, political, environmental, cultural, whatever – but these overarching values and goals of architecture will remain constants.

Introduction

1 The Villa Rotonda is also known as the Villa Almerico, after
   the retired Vatican official who started the project with
   Palladio, and as the Villa Capra after the new owner who
   completed the work with some modifications to the original
   design by Palladio's student Vincenzo Scamozzi (1548–1616).
   See Peter Murray, *The Architecture of the Italian Renaissance*
   (New York: Schocken Books, 1963), pp. 249–52, and Robert
   Tavernor, *Palladio and Palladianism* (London: Penguin, 1991),
   pp. 77–78.

2 On life in a Palladian villa, although in this case one that was
   also the headquarters of a working agricultural estate, the Villa
   Foscari owned by two wealthy Venetian brothers, see Antonio
   Foscari, *Living with Palladio in the Sixteenth Century* (Zürich:
   Lars Müller Publishers, 2020). For a charming account of his
   recent visits to several Palladian villas, see Witold Rybczynski,
   *The Perfect House: A Journey with the Renaissance Master
   Andrea Palladio* (New York: Scribner, 2002).

3 Quoted from Kenneth Frampton, *A Genealogy of Modern
   Architecture: Comparative Critical Analysis of Built Form*,
   edited by Ashley Simone (Zürich: Lars Müller Publishers,
   2015), p. 111.

4 Vitruvius, *On Architecture*, Book I, chapter iii, paragraph 2, in
   translation by Richard Schofield with introduction by Robert
   Tavernor (London: Penguin, 2009), p. 19; Vitruvius, *The Ten
   Books of Architecture*, translated by Morris Hicky Morgan
   (Cambridge, MA: Harvard University Press, 1914), Book I,

chapter iii, paragraph 2, p. 17. *Venustas* could also be translated as the quality of being charming, graceful, or attractive in appearance or style, or even being "lucky in love"; see *Oxford Latin Dictionary*, edited by P. G. W. Glare (Oxford: Clarendon Press, 1982, reprinted with corrections 1996), p. 2032.

5 Kenneth Frampton, *Studies in Tectonic Culture: The Poetics of Construction in Nineteenth and Twentieth Century Architecture*, edited by John Cava (Cambridge, MA: MIT Press, 1995), p. 85.

6 A. W. N. Pugin, *The True Principles of Pointed or Christian Architecture* (London: John Weale, 1843), p. 1, cited by Frampton, *Tectonic Culture*, p. 37.

7 Frampton, *Tectonic Culture*, p. 40.

8 "*Art, skill, craft in work, cunning of hand*, esp. of metal-working, *Odyssey*; of a shipwright, *Iliad*, of a soothsayer, Aeschylus, Sophocles ... *an art*, i.e. *a system* or *method of making or doing*, Plato, Aristotle"; *An Intermediate Greek-English Lexicon, founded upon the Seventh Edition of Liddell and Scott's Greek-English Lexicon* (Oxford: Clarendon Press, 1889), p. 804.

9 John Ruskin, *The Seven Lamps of Architecture* (1849), second edition (Orpington, UK: George Allen, 1880), chapter 1, p. 8.

10 There has been extensive discussion of whether in view of its practical purposes architecture can be counted as one of the "fine arts" and whether architects can count as "artists" like painters, sculptors, poets, or composers, but I do not intend to focus on these questions. For useful discussion, see Richard Hill, *Designs and their Consequences: Architecture and Aesthetics* (New Haven, CT, and London: Yale University Press, 1999), especially chapters 1, 2, and 8.

11 See the classic work by Nikolaus Pevsner, *A History of Building Types*, the A. W. Mellon Lectures in the Fine Arts 1970,

Bollingen Series xxxv, 19 (Princeton, NJ: Princeton University Press, 1976). Pevsner focused on public buildings, and did not include private homes in his survey of building types.

12 Arthur Schopenhauer, *The World as Will and Representation* (second edition of 1844), translated by E. F. J. Payne (Indian Hills, CO: The Falcon Wing's Press, 1958), volume I, §43, p. 214.

13 Selldorf Architects Editorial Team, *Selldorf Architects: Portfolio and Projects* (London: Phaidon, 2016), p. 192, photos and plans of project, pp. 192–99.

14 For a well-known argument that there is no distinct category of aesthetic appreciation, see George Dickie, *Art and the Aesthetic* (Ithaca, NY: Cornell University Press, 1974). For an argument that architecture should be counted as a fine art, see Hill, *Designs and their Consequences*. For the purposes of this essay I will assume that the category of the aesthetic is sufficiently well-defined to be contrasted to other concepts. The latter question may be important because of the Romantic conception of the autonomy of the artist that might come along with the inclusion of architecture among the fine arts. I will touch on that issue in passing.

Chapter 1

1 Vitruvius's work was apparently known in the Middle Ages, but became especially prominent after the humanist Poggio Bracciolini (1380–1459), who also discovered Lucretius's *De rerum naturae*, found a manuscript in the monastic library of St. Gallen, Switzerland. There were no illustrations in the manuscript. An Italian translation with illustrations by Andrea Palladio, edited by his patron Daniele Barbaro, was published in Venice in 1567; see Vitruvius, *On Architecture*, translated by Richard Schofield with introduction by Robert Tavernor (London: Penguin, 2009), p. x. On Bracciolini's rediscovery of

Lucretius, an important source for naturalism in the Renaissance, see Stephen Greenblatt, *The Swerve: How the World Became Modern* (New York: W. W. Norton, 2011).

2 Vitruvius, *On Architecture*, I.i.10, p. 10.

3 A fascinating evolutionary account of architecture can be found in Grant Hildebrand, *Origins of Architectural Pleasure* (Berkeley and Los Angeles: University of California Press, 1999). I will return to Hildebrand in Chapter 3.

4 Vitruvius, *On Architecture*, II.i.3, p. 38. See Joseph Rykwert, *On Adam's House in Paradise: The Idea of the Primitive Hut in Architectural History* (New York: Museum of Modern Art, 1972).

5 See the discussions of Marc-Antoine Laugier and Gottfried Semper later in this chapter and in the next.

6 Vitruvius, *On Architecture*, II.i.1, p. 37.

7 Vitruvius, *On Architecture*, II.i.2, p. 38.

8 Vitruvius, *On Architecture*, II.i.4–5, pp. 38–99.

9 Vitruvius, *On Architecture*, IV.ii.2, p. 93.

10 Vitruvius, *On Architecture*, I.ii.7, p. 18.

11 Vitruvius, *On Architecture*, VI.i.1–2, p. 166.

12 Vitruvius, *On Architecture*, I.iv.1, p. 20.

13 Vitruvius, *On Architecture*, IV.xii.1, p. 160.

14 Vitruvius, *On Architecture*, I.vi, pp. 27–33.

15 Vitruvius, *On Architecture*, I.vii.1, pp. 33–34.

16 Vitruvius, *On Architecture*, II.ii.1–2, p. 41.

17 Vitruvius, *On Architecture*, II.iii.1–4, pp. 42–43.

18 Vitruvius, *On Architecture*, II.iv–v, pp. 43–45.

19 Vitruvius, *On Architecture*, II.vi, pp. 45–47.

20 Vitruvius, *On Architecture*, II.vii, pp. 48–50.

21 Vitruvius, *On Architecture*, II.viii.1, p. 50.

22 Vitruvius, *On Architecture*, II.viii.16, p. 55.

23 Vitruvius, *On Architecture*, II.ix.6, p. 58.

24 Vitruvius, *On Architecture*, II.ix.10, pp. 59–60.

25 Vitruvius, *On Architecture*, II.ix.14, p. 61.

26 Vitruvius, *On Architecture*, II.x.3, p. 63.

27 Alexander Gottlieb Baumgarten, *Aesthetica*, volume 1 (1750), §1, modern edition edited by Dagmar Mirbach (Hamburg: Felix Meiner Verlag, 2007), volume 1, pp. 10–11. Baumgarten had already introduced the term in his dissertation *Meditationes philosophicae de nonnullis ad poema pertinentibus* (Philosophical meditations on some matters pertaining to poetry) (1735), §CXVI, modern edition edited by Heinz Paetzold (Hamburg: Felix Meiner Verlag, 1983), pp. 86–87.

28 Vitruvius, *On Architecture*, III.i.

29 Vitruvius, *The Ten Books of Architecture*, translated by Morris Hicky Morgan, Cambridge, MA: Harvard University Press, 1914), Book I, chapter ii, paragraph 1, p. 13; at least in the case of *eurythmia* and *symmetria* the Greek terms are just transliterated into Latin.

30 Vitruvius, *Ten Books*, I.ii.2, p. 13; *On Architecture*, I.ii.2, pp. 13–14.

31 Vitruvius, *On Architecture*, I.ii.2, p. 14.

32 Vitruvius, *On Architecture*, I.ii.2, p. 14.

33 Vitruvius, *On Architecture*, I.ii.3, p. 14.

34 Vitruvius, *On Architecture*, I.ii.5, p. 17.

35 Vitruvius, *On Architecture*, I.ii.6, p. 17.

36 Vitruvius, *On Architecture*, I.ii.7, p. 18.

37 Vitruvius, *On Architecture*, I.ii.8, p. 18.

38 Vitruvius, *On Architecture*, I.ii.9, pp. 18–19.

39 Vitruvius, *On Architecture*, III.i.4, p. 67.

40 Vitruvius, *On Architecture*, III.i.5, p. 67.

41 Vitruvius, *On Architecture*, III.i.7, p. 68.

42 Vitruvius, *On Architecture*, IV.i.6, p. 91.

43 Vitruvius, *On Architecture*, IV.i.8, p. 92.

44 Vitruvius, *On Architecture*, IV.i.8, p. 92.

45 Vitruvius, *On Architecture*, IV.i.9, p. 92.

46 Vitruvius, *On Architecture*, III.iii.13, p. 78.

47 Vitruvius, *On Architecture*, III.iii.11, p. 78.

48 Vitruvius, *On Architecture*, III.iv.5, p. 80.

49 Vitruvius, *On Architecture*, III.v.8, p. 85.

50 Vitruvius, *On Architecture*, III.iii.13, pp. 78–79.

51 Vitruvius, *On Architecture*, editor's note at p. 7.

52 Vitruvius, *On Architecture*, I.i.5, p. 6.

53 See Anthony Grafton, *Leon Battista Alberti: Master Builder of the Italian Renaissance* (New York: Hill & Wang, 2000).

54 Leon Battista Alberti, *On the Art of Building in Ten Books*, translated by Joseph Rykwert, Neil Leach, and Robert Tavernor (Cambridge, MA: MIT Press, 1988), Book I, section 2, p. 9.

55 Alberti, *Art of Building*, VI.2, p. 156.

56 Alberti, *Art of Building*, VI.2, p. 157.

57 Alberti, *Art of Building*, IX.5, p. 303.

58 Alberti, *Art of Building*, IX.5, p. 302.

59 Alberti, *Art of Building*, IX.5, p. 302.

60 Alberti, *Art of Building*, IX.5, p. 305.

61 Alberti, *Art of Building*, IX.7, p. 309.

62 Alberti, *Art of Building*, VII.6, p. 201.

63 Alberti, *Art of Building*, VII.9, p. 215.

64 Alberti, *Art of Building*, VI.1, p. 154.

65 See Sergio Villari, *J. N. L. Durand (1760–1834): Art and Science of Architecture*, translated by Eli Gottlieb (New York: Rizzoli, 1990).

66 Claude Perrault, *Ordonnance for the Five Kinds of Columns after the Method of the Ancients*, translated by Indra Kagis McEwen, introduction by Alberto Pérez-Gómez (Santa Monica: Getty Center, 1993).

67 Leon Battista Alberti, *On Painting*, translated by Cecil Grayson (London: Penguin, 1991), Book II, §30, p. 64.

68 See James S. Ackerman, *Palladio* (London: Penguin, 1966), p. 20.

69 See Ackerman, *Palladio*, pp. 50–57.

70 Ackerman, *Palladio*, pp. 130–32.

71 Ackerman, *Palladio*, pp. 160–70.

72 For surveys of the vast range of material I am omitting, see Hanno-Walter Kruft, *History of Architectural Theory from Vitruvius to the Present*, translated by Ronald Taylor, Elsie Callendar, and Antony Wood (New York: Princeton Architectural Press, 1994); Veronica Bierman et al., *Architectural Theory from the Renaissance to the Present* (Cologne: Taschen, 2003); and Harry Francis Mallgrave, ed., *Architectural Theory: Volume 1: An Anthology from Vitruvius to 1870* (Oxford: Blackwell, 2007).

73 Henry Home, Lord Kames, *Elements of Criticism* (1785), sixth edition; modern edition edited by Peter Jones, 2 volumes (Indianapolis: Liberty Fund, 2005), chapter XXIV, p. 699.

74 Kames, *Elements*, XXIV, p. 705.

75 Kames, *Elements*, XXIV, p. 715. Here, demonstrating his learning, Kames illustrates this point with the Hagia Sophia as described by the Byzantine historian Procopius (ca. 527–65 CE) in *De aedificiis* (ca. 555–60). See Jones's note 10, p. 715.

76 David Hume, *A Treatise of Human Nature* (1739–40), Book II, part I, §8, "Of Beauty and Deformity"; in the edition by David J. and Mary Fate Norton, 2 volumes (Oxford: Clarendon Press, 2007), volume 1, p. 195.

77 Kames, *Elements*, ch. XXIV, p. 700.

78 Kames, *Elements*, ch. XXIV, p. 701.

79 Kames, *Elements*, ch. XXIV, pp. 704–5.

80 Kames, *Elements*, ch. XXIV, p. 706.

81 Kames, *Elements*, ch. XXIV, p. 707.

82 Charles Batteux, *The Fine Arts Reduced to a Single Principle*, translated by James O. Young (Oxford: Oxford University Press, 2015).

83 Marc-Antoine Laugier, *An Essay on Architecture*, translated by Wolfgang and Anni Hermann (Los Angeles: Hennessey & Ingalls, 1977), p. v.

84 Laugier, *Essay on Architecture*, ch. I, pp. 12–13.

85 Laugier, *Essay on Architecture*, ch. i, article i, p. 19.

86 Laugier, *Essay on Architecture*, ch. iii, article i, pp. 68–81.

87 Laugier, *Essay on Architecture*, ch. iii, article ii, pp. 81–90, at p. 81.

88 Laugier, *Essay on Architecture*, ch. iii, article iii, pp. 90–99, at p. 90.

Chapter 2

1 Immanuel Kant, *Critique of the Power of Judgment*, edited by Paul Guyer, translated by Paul Guyer and Eric Matthews (Cambridge: Cambridge University Press, 2000), §2, 5:205; as is standard in Kant scholarship, pagination is given not by the page numbers of the translation but by volume (in this case volume 5) and page number of *Kant's gesammelte Schriften*, edited by the Royal Prussian (later German, then Berlin-Brandenburg) Academy of Sciences, 29 volumes (Berlin: Georg Reimer, later Walter de Gruyter, 1900–).

2 Kant, *Critique of the Power of Judgment*, §15, 5:226.

3 Kant, *Critique of the Power of Judgment*, §16, 5:229.

4 Kant, *Critique of the Power of Judgment*, §16, 5:229–30.

5 I have offered an overview of Kant's entire philosophy in *Kant*, second edition (London: Routledge, 2014). I have provided a detailed interpretation of the *Critique of Pure Reason* in *Kant and the Claims of Knowledge* (Cambridge: Cambridge University Press, 1987), and discussed Kant's moral philosophy in numerous works, most recently *Kant on the Rationality of Morality* (Cambridge: Cambridge University Press, 2019). My main work on Kant's aesthetics is *Kant and the Claims of Taste* (Cambridge, MA: Harvard University Press, 1979; second edition, Cambridge: Cambridge University Press, 1997).

6 The second half of the third critique, the "Critique of the Teleological Power of Judgment," concerns our judgments about organisms in nature and the purposiveness (*Zweckmäßigkeit*) of nature as a whole, rather than art.

7 Kant, *Critique of the Power of Judgment*, §1, 5:203–4.

8 Kant, *Critique of the Power of Judgment*, §§6–7, 5:211–13.

9 Kant, *Critique of the Power of Judgment*, Introduction, §vɪ, 5:185.

10 Kant, *Critique of the Power of Judgment*, §21, 5:238–39, and §38, 5:290–1.

11 Kant, *Critique of the Power of Judgment*, Introduction, §vɪɪ, 5:190.

12 Kant, *Critique of the Power of Judgment*, §14, 5:225. It is hard to believe that Kant did not have Alberti's theory of painting in mind here, whether directly or indirectly.

13 For a more detailed presentation of this interpretation, see my "The Harmony of the Faculties Revisited," in Guyer, *Values of Beauty: Historical Essays in Aesthetics* (Cambridge: Cambridge University Press, 2005), pp. 77–109.

14 Friedrich Nietzsche, *On the Genealogy of Morality*, translation by Carol Diethe, edited by Keith Ansell-Pearson (Cambridge: Cambridge University Press, revised edition 2007), third essay, §6, p. 74.

15 Kant, *Critique of the Power of Judgment*, §16, 5:229–30.

16 For a fuller discussion of Kant's contrast, see my "Free and Adherent Beauty: A Modest Proposal," *British Journal of Aesthetics* 42 (2002): 357–66, reprinted in *Values of Beauty*, pp. 129–40; for my interpretation of Kant on art, see "Kant's Conception of Art," *Journal of Aesthetics and Art Criticism* 52 (1994): 175–85, reprinted as chapter 12 of the second edition of my *Kant and the Claims of Taste*, pp. 351–66.

17 Kant, *Critique of the Power of Judgment*, §43, 5:303–4.

18 Kant, *Critique of the Power of Judgment*, §45, 5:306.

19 Kant, *Critique of the Power of Judgment*, §47, 5:309.

20 Kant, *Critique of the Power of Judgment*, §49, 5:318.

21 Kant, *Critique of the Power of Judgment*, §49, 5:314.

22 Kant, *Critique of the Power of Judgment*, §52, p. 326.

23 Kant, *Critique of the Power of Judgment*, §51, 5:320.

24 Kant, *Critique of the Power of Judgment*, §51, 5:322.

25 Kant, *Metaphysics of Morals*, Doctrine of Right, Introduction, §C, 6:230; in Kant, *Practical Philosophy*, edited and translated by Mary J. Gregor (Cambridge: Cambridge University Press, 1996), p. 387; for the formula of humanity, see Kant, *Groundwork for the Metaphysics of Morals*, 4:428–29; in *Practical Philosophy*, pp. 79–80. In the case of Kant, the references in the form "n:nn", e.g. "4:428–9," refer to the volume and page numbers as in the standard German edition of Kant, the "Academy edition" (*Kant's gesammelte Schriften*, edited by the Royal Prussian [later German, then Berlin-Brandenburg] Academy of Sciences, Berlin: Georg Reimer [later Walter de Gruyter & Co.], 29 vols, 1900–).

26 Hegel offered a strictly intellectualist, meaning-based approach to architecture as the most symbolic and therefore most primitive form of art in his *Aesthetics: Lectures on the Fine Arts*, translated by T. M. Knox, 2 volumes (Oxford: Clarendon Press, 1975); for a shorter version, see Hegel, *Lectures on the Philosophy of Art: The Hotho Transcript of the 1823 Berlin Lectures,* translated by Robert F. Brown (Oxford: Clarendon Press, 2014). But Schopenhauer's transition from a cognitivist approach to a structural-functionalist aesthetics of architecture will be of more interest in the argument of this book. The nineteenth-century architect and theorist Eugène-Emmanuel Viollet-le-Duc (1814–79) distinguished between "two indispensable ways in which truth must be adhered to" in architecture, "true in respect of the programme and true in respect of the constructive progress," the first fulfilling "exactly, scrupulously, the conditions imposed" by the program for the building, the second employing "the materials according to their qualities and properties"; *Discourses on Architecture*, translated by B. Bucknell (London: George Allen

& Unwin, 1959), p. 448, cited from Edward Winters, *Aesthetics and Architecture* (London: Continuum, 2007), p. 40.

27 Arthur Schopenhauer, *The World as Will and Representation* (1844), second edition, §51; translated by E. F. J. Payne (Indian Springs, CO: The Falcon's Wing Press, 1958), volume I, p. 250.

28 Schopenhauer, *World as Will and Representation*, §43, vol. I, p. 214.

29 Schopenhauer, *World as Will and Representation*, §43, vol. I, pp. 214–15.

30 Schopenhauer, *World as Will and Representation*, supplementary chapter XXXV (1844), vol. II, p. 411.

31 Schopenhauer, *World as Will and Representation*, ch. XXXV, vol. II, p. 416.

32 Schopenhauer, *World as Will and Representation*, ch. XXXV, vol. II, pp. 416–17.

33 Schopenhauer, *World as Will and Representation*, §43, vol. I, p. 215. Cp. Marc-Antoine Laugier, *An Essay on Architecture*, translated by Wolfgang and Anni Hermann (Los Angeles: Hennessey & Ingalls, 1977), chapter I, article I, pp. 14–22. Laugier had animadverted against both twisted columns and pilasters that they did not imitate the pure round form of the original tree-trunk corner-posts of the primitive hut.

34 Schopenhauer, *World as Will and Representation*, ch. XXXV, vol. II, p. 412.

35 For the problem with flat roofs, see Stewart Brand, *How Buildings Learn: What Happens After They're Built* (New York: Penguin Books, 1994), pp. 58, 115.

36 *The Complete Works of John Ruskin: The Library Edition*, edited by E. T. Cook and Alexander Wedderburn (London: George Allen and Unwin, 1903–12).

37 For my approach to Ruskin's place in the history of aesthetics, see Guyer, *A History of Modern Aesthetics*, volume 2, *The Nineteenth Century* (Cambridge: Cambridge University Press, 2014), pp. 191–228. For my previous interpretation of Ruskin's work on

architecture, see my "Monism and Pluralism in the Philosophy of Architecture," part I, *Architecture Philosophy* 1/1 (2014): 25–42, and "Monism and Pluralism in the Philosophy of Architecture," part II, *Architecture Philosophy* 1/2 (2015): 231–44.

38 John Ruskin, *The Seven Lamps of Architecture* (Orpington, UK: George Allen, 1880), p. 3.

39 Ruskin, *Seven Lamps*, p. 9.

40 Ruskin, *Seven Lamps*, p. 8.

41 Ruskin, *Seven Lamps*, pp. 9–10.

42 Ruskin, *Seven Lamps*, p. 10.

43 Ruskin, *Seven Lamps*, p. 11.

44 Ruskin, *Seven Lamps*, p. 34.

45 Ruskin, *Seven Lamps*, p. 35.

46 Ruskin, *Seven Lamps*, p. 37.

47 Ruskin, *Seven Lamps*, p. 39.

48 Although whether or not he knew Kant, Ruskin would surely have known Edmund Burke's 1757 *Philosophical Enquiry into the Origin of Our Ideas of the Sublime and Beautiful*, edited by Paul Guyer (Oxford: Oxford University Press, 2015).

49 Ruskin, *Seven Lamps*, pp. 72–73.

50 Ruskin, *Seven Lamps*, p. 73.

51 Ruskin, *Seven Lamps*, p 77.

52 Ruskin, *Seven Lamps*, p. 81.

53 Ruskin, *Seven Lamps*, p. 83.

54 Ruskin, *Seven Lamps*, p. 84.

55 Ruskin, *Seven Lamps*, p. 85.

56 Ruskin, *Seven Lamps*, p. 103.

57 Ruskin, *Seven Lamps*, p. 104.

58 Here Ruskin is surely following the line of thought developed by the most committed associationist of eighteenth-century British associationists, namely Archibald Alison, author of *Essays on the Nature and Principles of Taste* (1790, with a second edition in 1811, thus not long before Ruskin's birth). For

discussions of Alison, see George Dickie, *The Century of Taste* (New York: Oxford University Press, 1996), and Guyer, *A History of Modern Aesthetics*, volume 1, *The Eighteenth Century* (Cambridge: Cambridge University Press, 2014), pp. 226–35.

59 Ruskin, *Seven Lamps*, pp. 148–49.

60 Ruskin, *Seven Lamps*, p. 152.

61 Ruskin, *Seven Lamps*, p. 178.

62 Ruskin, *Seven Lamps*, pp. 186–87.

63 Ruskin, *Seven Lamps*, p. 205.

64 Ruskin, *Seven Lamps*, p. 200.

65 John Ruskin, "The Nature of Gothic," in John Ruskin, *Selected Writings*, edited by Dinah Birch (Oxford: Oxford University Press, 2004), pp. 32–63, at pp. 33–35.

66 Ruskin, "The Nature of Gothic," pp. 38–39.

67 Ruskin, "The Nature of Gothic," p. 43; Ruskin's critique of the effects of the division of labor follows in the tradition of such works as Adam's Smith's *The Wealth of Nations* (1776) and Friedrich Schiller's *Letters on the Aesthetic Education of Mankind* (1795), although he writes without Smith's recognition that the division of labor has benefits as well as costs.

68 Ruskin, "The Nature of Gothic," p. 39.

69 Ruskin, "The Nature of Gothic," p. 42.

70 Ruskin, "The Nature of Gothic," p. 55.

71 Gottfried Semper, *The Four Elements of Architecture and Other Writings*, translated by Harry Francis Mallgrave and Wolfgang Herrmann, with introduction by Joseph Rykwert (Cambridge: Cambridge University Press, 1989), pp. 74–129.

72 Translated by Harry Francis Mallgrave (Los Angeles: Getty Publications, 2004); selections in *Four Elements*, pp. 181–263.

73 Semper, *Four Elements*, p. 103.

74 Semper, *Four Elements*, p. 103.

75 Semper, *Four Elements*, p. 103.

76 Semper, *Four Elements*, p. 104.

77 Semper, *Four Elements*, p. 123.

NOTES TO PAGES 98–102

Chapter 3

1 On this distinction see my 2011 Presidential Address to the
American Society for Aesthetics, "Monism and Pluralism in
the History of Aesthetics," *Journal of Aesthetics and Art
Criticism* 71 (2013): 133–43, and more generally my *A History of
Modern Aesthetics*, 3 volumes (Cambridge: Cambridge
University Press, 2014).

2 For a convincing argument that function can never fully
determine form, especially because it is difficult to pin
down precisely what the intended use of a building is, see
Richard Hill, *Designs and their Consequences: Architecture
and Aesthetics* (New Haven, CT, and London: Yale
University Press, 1999), chapter 7. In Chapter 4 below, we
will see that Mies van der Rohe built his later practice
around the idea that any building could have multiple
functions over its life, often not foreseeable at the time of
its design and construction.

3 Louis Sullivan, *The Autobiography of an Idea* (New York:
Dover, 1956), p. 234, cited from Albert Bush-Brown, *Louis
Sullivan* (New York: George Braziller, 1960), p. 8.

4 William J. R. Curtis, *Modern Architecture since 1900*, third
edition (London: Phaidon, 1996), p. 7.

5 Curtis, *Modern Architecture*, pp. 11–12.

6 John Summerson, *The Classical Language of Architecture*
(Cambridge, MA: MIT Press, 1965).

7 For criticism of the metaphor of architectural language, see
Roger Scruton, *Aesthetics and Architecture* (Princeton, NJ:
Princeton University Press, 1979), chapter 7; Hill, *Designs and
their Consequences*, chapter 5; and Edward Winters, *Aesthetics
and Architecture* (London: Continuum, 2007), chapter 11. With
reference to the structuralist Ferdinand de Saussure and his
followers, Winters writes that "It is because we are concerned

with the experience of works of architecture – and with the meaning of architecture only insofar as that enters into our experience – that we must forego [*sic*] the structuralists' claims that language provides a suitable model with which to compare our understanding of architecture" (pp. 127–28).

8 Rafael Moneo, *Theoretical Anxiety and Design Strategies in the Work of Eight Contemporary Architects* (Cambridge, MA: MIT Press, 2004), pp. 148–49.

9 Robert Venturi, Denise Scott Brown, and Steven Izenour, *Learning from Las Vegas: The Forgotten Symbolism of Architectural Form* (Cambridge, MA: MIT Press, 1972), pp. 88, 80.

10 See Nelson Goodman, *Languages of Art* (Indianapolis: Bobbs-Merrill, 1968), and his application of his approach to architecture in "How Buildings Mean," *Critical Inquiry* 11 (1985), final version in Nelson Goodman and Catherine Z. Elgin, *Reconceptions in Philosophy and Other Arts and Sciences* (Indianapolis: Hackett Publishing Co., 1988), pp. 31–48.

11 Susanne K. Langer, *Philosophy in a New Key: A Study in the Symbolism of Reason, Rite, and Art* (Cambridge, MA: Harvard University Press, 1942), and Langer, *Feeling and Form* (New York: Scribner's, 1953).

12 Langer, *Feeling and Form*, p. 212.

13 Langer, *Feeling and Form*, p. 92.

14 Langer, *Feeling and Form*, p. 93.

15 Langer, *Feeling and Form*, p. 94.

16 Langer, *Feeling and Form*, p. 95.

17 Langer, *Feeling and Form*, p. 95.

18 Langer, *Feeling and Form*, p. 97.

19 Langer, *Feeling and Form*, p. 213.

20 See Langer's Plates i through ix between pp. 208 and 209 of *Feeling and Form*.

21 Langer, *Feeling and Form*, p. 404.

22 The most recent English translation is G. W. F. Hegel, *The Phenomenology of Spirit*, translated with commentary by Michael Inwood (Oxford: Oxford University Press, 2018).

23 In Martin Heidegger, *Off the Beaten Track*, translated by Julian Young and Kenneth Haynes (Cambridge: Cambridge University Press, 2002), pp. 1–56.

24 Martin Heidegger, "Bauen Wohnen Denken," in *Darmstadter Gespräch Mensch und Raum* (Darmstadt: Darmstädter Verlagsanstalt, 1952), pp. 72–84, translated in Heidegger, *Poetry, Language, Thought*, translated by Albert Hofstadter (New York: Harper & Row, 1971), pp. 145–61.

25 Christian Norberg-Schulz, *The Concept of Dwelling: On the Way to Figurative Architecture* (New York: Rizzoli International, 1985).

26 Maurice Merleau-Ponty, *The Phenomenology of Perception*, translated by D. Landes (London: Routledge, 2012); see Fred Rush, *On Architecture* (London: Routledge, 2009), especially chapter 1, "Bodies and Architectural Space," pp. 1–54.

27 Steen Eiler Rasmussen, *Experiencing Architecture*, translated by Eve Wendt (Cambridge, MA: MIT Press, 1959, 1964).

28 Rasmussen, *Experiencing Architecture*, p. 9.

29 Rasmussen, *Experiencing Architecture*, p. 10.

30 Rasmussen, *Experiencing Architecture*, p. 14.

31 Rasmussen, *Experiencing Architecture*, p. 33.

32 Rasmussen, *Experiencing Architecture*, p. 36.

33 Immanuel Kant, *Critique of the Power of Judgment*, edited by Paul Guyer, translated by Paul Guyer and Eric Matthews (Cambridge: Cambridge University Press, 2000), §8, 5:216.

34 John Ruskin, *The Seven Lamps of Architecture* (1849), second edition (Orpington, UK: George Allen, 1880), p. 208.

35 Grant Hildebrand, *Origins of Architectural Pleasure* (Berkeley and Los Angeles: University of California Press, 1999).

36 Here Hildebrand follows Jay Appleton, *The Experience of Landscape* (1975; revised edition London: Wiley, 1996).

37 Two other applications of evolutionary theory to aesthetics, although not specifically to architecture, both published after Hildebrand's book and thus not cited by him, are Dennis Dutton, *The Art Instinct: Beauty, Pleasure, and Human Evolution* (London: Bloomsbury, 2009), and Stephen Davies, *The Artful Species: Aesthetics, Art, and Evolution* (Oxford: Oxford University Press, 2013).

38 Grant Hildebrand, *The Wright Space: Pattern and Meaning in Frank Lloyd Wright's Houses* (Seattle: University of Washington Press, 1991).

39 Hildebrand, *The Wright Space*, pp. 42–43.

40 See the diagrams at Hildebrand, *The Wright Space*, pp. 44, 55.

41 Hildebrand, *The Wright Space*, p. 36.

42 Scruton, *Aesthetics of Architecture*. Scruton's well-known political conservatism, his preference for classical style, and his association with Prince Charles in that regard, will not concern us here; for that, see his volume *The Classical Vernacular: Architectural Principles in an Age of Nihilism* (Manchester: Carcanet Press, 1994).

43 Scruton, *Aesthetics of Architecture*, ch. 9.

44 Scruton, *Aesthetics of Architecture*, pp. 94–95.

45 See Peter Murray, *The Architecture of the Italian Renaissance* (New York: Schocken Books, 1963), p. 154. Murray offers a detailed description of this building, the "last and greatest work" of its architect, pp. 153–58.

46 Scruton, *Aesthetics of Architecture*, pp. 87–88.

47 *Anchoring, Intertwining, Parallax,* and *Compression* all New York: Princeton Architectural Press; *Color, Light and Time* and *Scale* are Zürich: Lars Mueller Publishers.

48 Robert McCarter, *Steven Holl* (London: Phaidon, 2015), p. 78.

49 McCarter, *Steven Holl*, p. 79.

50 Steven Holl, *Anchoring* (New York: Princeton Architectural Press, 1989), pp. 66–69.

Chapter 4

1   Frank Lloyd Wright, "In the Cause of Architecture [II]," *Architectural Record* (May, 1914): 405–13, at p. 405.

2   Frank Lloyd Wright, "In the Cause of Architecture [I]," *Architectural Record* (March, 1908): 155–65, at p. 156.

3   In early Prairie School houses, this was typically the ground floor; in later ones, it was often the second floor, so the rooms could have cathedral ceilings; perhaps Wright originated that now-common American ceiling as well.

4   Wright, "In the Cause of Architecture [I]," p. 156.

5   Wright, "In the Cause of Architecture [I]," p. 157.

6   Wright, "In the Cause of Architecture [II]," p. 413.

7   William H. Jordy, *American Buildings and their Architects: Progressive and Academic Ideals at the Turn of the Twentieth Century* (Garden City, NY: Anchor Books, 1976), p. 206.

8   Frank Lloyd Wright, *When Democracy Builds* (Chicago: The University of Chicago Press, 1945), p. 124, cited from Gwendolyn Wright, "Frank Lloyd Wright and the Domestic Landscape," in *Frank Lloyd Wright Architect*, edited by Terence Riley (New York: Museum of Modern Art, 1994), pp. 80–95, at p. 90.

9   As Peter Blake wrote, "It is almost impossible to catalogue the infinite number of innovations in residential architecture which accompanied Wright's development of the Prairie house" – ribbon, corner, and casement windows, cathedral ceilings, concrete-slab floors with radiant heating, built-in lighting, and more, much of which we now take completely for granted; *The Master Builders* (New York: Alfred A. Knopf, 1960), p. 300. But the available technology often made it hard to repair the heating or change the bulbs.

10 See the detailed account of the construction of the Guggenheim in William H. Jordy, *American Buildings and their Architects: The Impact of European Modernism in the*

Mid-Twentieth Century (Garden City, NY: Anchor Books, 1976), chapter v, pp. 279–360.

11 Wright, "In the Cause of Architecture [1]," p. 162. In this passage Wright uses the phrase "family resemblance" long before Ludwig Wittgenstein's *Philosophical Investigations* (1953) made it ubiquitous.

12 But for his positive assessment of Wagner, see "Otto Wagner" (1911), in Adolf Loos, *On Architecture*, edited by Adolf Opel, translated by Michael Mitchell (Riverside, CA: Ariadne Press, 2002), pp. 86–91. See also Werner Oechslin, *Otto Wagner, Adolf Loos, and the Road to Modern Architecture*, translated by Lynette Widder (Cambridge: Cambridge University Press, 1994).

13 *Ausgeführte Bauten und Entwürfe von Frank Lloyd Wright* (Executed Buildings and Designs by Frank Lloyd Wright) and *Frank Lloyd Wright: Ausgeführte Bauten* (Frank Lloyd Wright: Executed Buildings) (Berlin: Ernst Wasmuth, 1910–11).

14 Loos even attempted his own journal on design and society, *Das Andere: Ein Blatt zu Einführung abendlaendischer Kultur in Oesterreich* (The Other: A Journal for the Introduction of Western Culture into Austria), which lasted for exactly two numbers in 1903 (reprint with translation, Zürich: Lars Müller Publishers, 2016).

15 For Loos's own account of the building, see "My Building on Michaelerplatz" (1911), in *On Architecture*, pp. 92–107.

16 An extensive catalogue of Loos's buildings, with plans and elevations, original and recent photographs, and details about construction as well as the original clients, is Ralf Bock, *Adolf Loos: Works and Projects* (Turin: Skira, 2007).

17 Adolf Loos, "Architecture" (1910), *On Architecture*, pp. 73–85, at p. 82.

18 For the complicated history of this essay, see Christopher Long, *Essays on Adolf Loos* (Prague: Karel Kerlický–KANT, 2019), chapter 2, "The Origin and Meanings of 'Ornament and Crime'," pp. 53–89.

19 Loos, "Ornament and Crime," in *Ornament and Crime: Selected Essays*, translated by Michael Mitchell (Riverside, CA: Ariadne Press, 1998), pp. 167–76, at p. 167; see also "Architecture," p. 75.

20 See Immanuel Kant, *Critique of the Power of Judgment*, edited by Paul Guyer, translated by Paul Guyer and Eric Matthews (Cambridge: Cambridge University Press, 2000), §16, 5:230.

21 Loos, "Ornament and Crime," p. 169.

22 See Christian Witt-Düring, ed., *Josef Hoffman: Interiors 1902–1913* (New York: Neue Galerie, and Munich: Prestel, 2006).

23 Loos, "Ornament and Crime," pp. 169–70.

24 Loos, "Ornament and Crime," pp. 170–71.

25 Loos, "Ornament and Crime," p. 174.

26 Loos, "Architecture," p. 82.

27 Loos, "Poor Little Rich Man," in Loos, *On Architecture*, pp. 47–52, at p. 48.

28 Loos, "Poor Little Rich Man," p. 51.

29 See Detlef Mertins, *Mies* (London: Phaidon, 2014), p. 236.

30 Cited in Jordy, *American Buildings and their Architects: The Impact of European Modernism in the Mid-Twentieth Century*, p. 221.

31 On the influence of Guardini, see Mertins, *Mies*, especially pp. 147–60; on Heidegger, see pp. 178–79.

32 Mies, "Schön und praktisch bauen! Schluß mit der kalten Zweckmäßigkeit" (Build beautifully and practically! Enough with cold functionality), *Duisburger General Anzeiger*, January 26, 1930, p. 2, in Mies van der Rohe, *Das kunstlose Wort: Gedanken zur Baukunst,* edited by Fritz Neumeyer, second edition (Berlin: DOM, 2016), p. 371.

33 Mies, "A Chapel: Illinois Institute of Architecture," *Arts and Architecture* 70 (1953): 18-19; *Das kunstlose Wort*, p. 393.

34 Mies, "Die Vorraussetzungen baukünstlicherische Schaffens," in *Das kunstloses Wort*, pp. 363–67, at p. 367. Mertins, *Mies*,

p. 135, quotes from the English translation of *Das kunstloses Wort*, but this is my translation from the original.

35 Grete Tugendhat, letter to *Die Form* 11 (November 15, 1931): 437–38, quoted from Mertins, *Mies*, p. 175.

36 Mertins, *Mies*, pp. 178–79.

37 Christian Norberg-Schulz, "A Talk with Mies van der Rohe," *Baukunst und Werkform* 11 (1958): 615–18, cited from Mertins, *Mies*, p. 266.

38 Peter Carter, *Mies van der Rohe at Work* (New York: Praeger, 1974), p. 37, quoted from Mertins, *Mies*, p. 266.

39 Mies, *Das kunstlose Wort*, p. 371.

40 See Tim Abrahams, "French Toast," *Architectural Record* (May, 2020): 60–67.

Chapter 5

1 G. W. F. Hegel, *Elements of the Philosophy of Right*, edited by Allen W. Wood, translated by H. B. Nisbet (Cambridge: Cambridge University Press, 1991), preface, pp. 23, 21–22.

2 See Chapter 3, note 37.

3 Alexander Nehamas, *Only a Promise of Happiness: The Place of Beauty in a World of Art* (Princeton, NJ: Princeton University Press, 2007).

4 Joseph Addison, "The Pleasures of the Imagination," *The Spectator* 411 (Saturday, June 21, 1712), in Addison, *The Spectator*, edited by Donald F. Bond (Oxford: Clarendon Press, 1965), volume III, pp. 535–36; for discussion, see Guyer, *A History of Modern Aesthetics*, volume 1, *The Eighteenth Century* (Cambridge: Cambridge University Press, 2014), pp. 63–73.

5 Alexander Gerard, *An Essay on Taste* (London and Edinburgh: A. Millar, A. Kincaid, and J. Bell, 1759), p. iii; see Guyer, *A History of Modern Aesthetics*, vol. 1, pp. 157–75.

6 John Ruskin, *The Seven Lamps of Architecture* (1849), second edition (Orpington, UK: George Allen, 1880), p. 39.

7 Joann Gonchar, "A New Lease on Life: The Renovation of a Storied Eero Saarinen Building Brings a Bit of the City to Suburbia," *Architectural Record* 2 (February, 2020): 74–81.

8 Cited from "Herzog and de Meuron," Wikipedia, accessed August 21, 2020.

9 See Josephine Minutillo, Tim Abrahams, Andrew Ayers, and Lydia Lee, "Building Type Study 1,019: Health Care," *Architectural Record* 7 (July, 2020): 67–90, and James S. Russell, "Designs that Heal Ruptures in Spaces We Share," *New York Times*, September 12, 2020.

10 "Leadership in Energy and Environmental Design," Wikipedia, accessed August 22, 2020.

11 Miriam Sitz, "Paul R. Williams's Archive Finds Home with USC and Getty," *Architectural Record* 8 (August, 2020): 16. A standard work, Rayner Banham, *Los Angeles: The Architecture of Four Ecologies* (London: Allen Lane, 1971), makes no mention of Williams.

12 See Richard Rothstein, *The Color of Law: The Forgotten History of How Our Government Segregated America* (New York: Liveright, 2017).

13 All these articles are in *Architectural Record* 10 (October, 2018).

14 See again Russell, "Designs that Heal."

15 Phil Bernstein, "Fast Forward: Architecture in 2031," *Architectural Record* 8 (August, 2020): 34.

INDEX